Techno
Vision

The Executive's Survival Guide to Understanding and Managing Information Technology

Charles B. Wang

McGraw-Hill, Inc.

New York   San Francisco   Washington, D.C.   Auckland   Bogotá
Caracas   Lisbon   London   Madrid   Mexico City   Milan
Montreal   New Delhi   San Juan   Singapore
Sydney   Tokyo   Toronto

Library of Congress Cataloging-in-Publication Data
Wang, Charles B.
    Techno Vision : the executive's survival guide to understanding
and managing information technology / by Charles B. Wang.
        p.   cm.
    Includes index.
    ISBN 0–07–068155–4 (acid-free paper)
    1. Information technology—Management. 2. Information resources
management. 3. Information storage and retrieval systems—
Management. I. Title.
HC79.I55W36   1994
658.4'038—dc20   94–19951
                                                           CIP

1 2 3 4 5 6 7 8 9 0   DOC/DOC   9 0 9 8 7 6 5 4

ISBN 0-07-068155-4

*The sponsoring editor for this book was Philip Ruppel, the
editing supervisor was Fred Dahl, and the production
supervisor was Donald F. Schmidt. It was set in Palatino
by Inkwell Publishing Services.*

Printed and bound by R. R. Donnelley & Sons Company.

This book is printed on recycled, acid-free paper
containing a minimum of 50 percent recycled
de-inked fiber.

Contents

A Special
Acknowledgment

I first and foremost want to extend my heartfelt thanks to John Kador. John enjoys a well-earned reputation as a talented journalist and wordsmith. A keen and enthusiastic observer of the information technology industry, whose special strength is expressing complex issues in terms anyone can understand, John worked closely with me to ensure that *Techno Vision* would be accessible to the lay reader as well as meaningful for the technologically annointed.

John has my great appreciation for the tremendous assistance he provided me in evolving this book to a completed manuscript.

Additional Acknowledgments

You know by my name that English is my second language. But what you may not know is that COBOL is my first. Technology is my passion. I like talking about it and I like working with it.

But to create a book like *Techno Vision* requires another dimension. It requires seeing the technology through the eyes of business managers and for that purpose, two people deserve special thanks.

First, it was Mary Welch who gave the book that added dimension. She, like me, is a technologist, but she added the images and expanded the descriptions so that business realities and technology are well balanced. Hers is a rare skill. It was through Mary's involvement in every aspect of this project—even before we knew it was a book—that *Techno Vision* took shape. I am convinced that without her tireless efforts, this book would still be another worthwhile project on a chief executive's "to do" list.

Second, it was in conversation with David Rothkopf, former chairman of The CEO Institutes and now Undersecretary of International Affairs at the Department of Commerce, that the original idea for this book germinated. As much as I attempted to overlook that conversation, he continued to remind me. I owe a great deal to David's persistence.

I also want to acknowledge the contributions of Bob Gordon and Beth Bloom whose careful reading of the manuscript helped ensure that this book be as coherent and cohesive as possible.

Finally, I owe a great deal of gratitude to all the CEOs and CIOs who have helped me define the disconnect. Without them, this book would not have been written.

Preface:
Why I Wrote Techno
Vision

Wandering between two worlds, one dead,
The other powerless to be born.
MATTHEW ARNOLD
British poet and critic, 1822–1888

Back in the early eighties when I was the thirty-something-year-old CEO of a $50-million software company, I started noticing a dynamic that made me profoundly uncomfortable.

I saw it first as an uneasy alliance between the senior executives responsible for managing organizations and the information technology people they hired to operate the organization's computers. In time, I watched that unease turn to frustration, occasional fury, and, worst of all for any human being, resignation. It saddened me that computer technology—the most liberating tool human beings have ever developed—could be the focus of so much anxiety and distress. I determined to understand this disturbing dynamic. I wanted to see if others shared my frustrations with information technology.

They did. The pain that business executives and information technology managers related to me was uncommonly similar. The stories I heard from hundreds of CEOs, managers, and technical professionals working in dozens of different disciplines persuaded me that a fundamental dynamic was operating. I doubled my efforts to make sense of the frustration I encountered. Finally it came to me.

Addressing an international conference of CEOs in 1992, I noticed that the temperature in the room invariably rose whenever the subject of information technology came up. Generally, these forums are characterized by a thoughtful, dignified, polite exchange of information and ideas. But when the discussion turned to information technology, the mood changed. I noticed that many of the senior executives—rational, calm, confident, self-controlled people comfortable with conflict—became almost raucous. People were angry, confused, intimidated, frustrated.

What, I thought to myself, is going on here? What is it that's so disturbing to these senior executives? Why are they so frustrated with information technology and the people who manage it? In the next few months, I went out of my way to observe encounters between business executives and information technologists. I listened to how they communicated and after a while I got it.

They're not talking to each other. They're talking *at* each other. They're talking *around* each other. It is nothing less than a fundamental disconnect between the technology executive and the rest of corporate management, a mismatch caused by disparities in training and temperament. The disconnect is so ingrained in corporate culture, that many organizations no longer recognize it as the profound limitation it represents to American productivity and competitiveness.

They're not talking to each other. It was painfully obvious that the people running the business and the people in charge of the information technology supposedly supporting the business didn't have the faintest idea of what the other side was talking about. The executives were talking about customers, world-class service, global competition, and return on investment. The information people seemed fixated on platforms, client/server computing, and object orientation. I was stunned. The two parties lacked a basic vocabulary to have a meaningful dialogue.

They're not talking to each other. The penalties are beyond calculation. Customer service, perhaps the key business measure of the last decade of the 1900s, is one such cost. Consider what CEOs have to say about the importance of information technology in developing products and services that meet customer expectations. In Japan, where, for many reasons, the

disconnect between senior management and information technology evolved differently, 49 percent of Japanese businesses
said that information technology is of primary importance in
meeting customer expectations, according to Tom Peters in *Liberation Management*. Only 22 percent of U.S. businesses could say
the same. That difference is one clear measure of the cost of the
disconnect; America's $65-billion balance of trade deficit with
Japan is another.

They're not talking to each other. I decided to see if I could act
as an interpreter. After all, I thought to myself, I run a successful
business so I know the business issues. The executives will listen
to me. Moreover, I head up a software company, and technology
is my background and my passion. The information technology
people will listen to me. Maybe all they need is a reminder that
they are on the same side and that, like the British and Ameri-
cans, they are a people separated by a common language.

They're not talking to each other. The gulf between the executives
and the information technologists was worse than I anticipated.
My early attempts to act as a polite go-between were met with
a mood I can only describe as a polite go-to-hell. Though I didn't
take it personally, I was saddened that the disconnect between
the corporate and technology executives could be so accepted
and even defended. I decided then to do something about
bringing these two sides together. I could no longer ignore the
terrible costs of watching the two sides shoot at each other across
a no-man's land of misinformation and ignorance.

They're not talking to each other. One of my objectives in writing
Techno Vision is to foster communication between the corporate
executive and technical management: to add my voice to eliminating the disconnect between finance-oriented executives and
technically-oriented managers. Its lessons are distilled from
three decades as a CEO in the software industry and, more
recently, from a series of conferences that brought senior executives and information technology people together for discussions of unprecedented candor. These ongoing conferences,
sponsored by Computer Associates International and The CEO
Institutes, have proven to be surprisingly successful in helping

senior executives and information technologists learn each others' vocabulary, share their legitimate concerns, and reclaim their inherent alliance in support of the business enterprises that sustain us all.

In the sixties, I was taught that if you're not part of the solution, you're part of the problem. I cringe to recall just how enthusiastically I may have been part of the disconnect. Early in my career I identified myself too strongly as a technician. I spoke too fast and glibly, using jargon I thought everyone should understand. Arrogantly, I assumed that my company's persuasive profits gave me license to speak and protected me from having to listen. I have been guilty at one time or another of a majority of the lapses this book documents.

I have come to learn a better way. *Techno Vision* is my heartfelt attempt to document what I have learned about how the relationship between executives and technologists developed and, more important, what the reader can do to reverse its effects. The book you're holding extracts the critical dimensions of my experience in managing information technologists, bridging the gulf between corporate management and technical executives, demystifying some of the bewildering changes occurring in information technology, and aligning that technology with the best hopes of people struggling to create productive, fulfilling careers.

Charles B. Wang
Islandia, New York

How to
Read This Book

This is a book about minding your business. It is written for chief executives and those who aspire to be. Whether you are a general executive or a manager in a company's information technology effort, you can approach this book on a number of levels.

First, *Techno Vision* outlines the reasons—both historical and temperamental—for the dysfunctional partnership between the business and technical managers of the enterprise and, more important, offers several prescriptions for repairing the alliance.

- Part I, "The Disconnect," explores the reasons that have led to the present situation.
- Part II, "Realignment," tackles the issue of realigning the information technology function with the business.
- Part III, "Information Technologies," summarizes the technologies that I consider most relevant to CEOs and attempts to put them into context.
- Part IV, "Connect," outlines a structural and attitudinal vision in which corporate vision and information technology are optimally aligned.

Second, the book serves as a reality check on the bewildering world of information technology. As a technologist myself, I know only too well the strengths and weaknesses of the technology initiatives of the last 20 years. You've heard them all: client/server, CASE, object-orientation. But you've never heard it like this. *Techno Vision* will help you cut through the fog and the hype, so that you can deal with what's really going on. Some people call a spade a spade. I call it a shovel. I take no prisoners in my judgment of the myriad technologies competing for your attention. Filtered through a sensibility jaundiced by too over-sold and underdelivered technologies, this section will help you manage your information effectively, without being intimidated.

Finally, the book summarizes the lessons I have drawn from a series of unique conferences called "The CEO in a Wired World." These technology boot camps bring together in an informal setting a small number of CEOs and a large mass of information technology. Everyone associated with these conferences has found them truly revelatory. These lessons are summarized in Chap. 12.

Readers, like me, who start a book from the back and flip through looking for items of interest, might appreciate various bite-sized blocks of information peppering each section. Since it is impossible to write a book about information technology without frequently pausing to explain a concept or define a term, I decided to pull most commentary out of the main text and position it as readings convenient to the place where it would otherwise appear.

Readers who stop at particular points in a text—whether attracted out of curiosity or a need for levity—can find nearby ruminations ranging from humorous to thoughtful. *Techno Vision* is thus designed for readers who bounce from chapter to chapter and welcome short readings. All explicitly labeled, the readings come in the following varieties:

[Anecdote] Most of the anecdotes included here describe authentic events that I have personally experienced. In a few cases, the anecdotes were recounted to me by colleagues at Computer Associates, CA clients, or business associates in the information technology industry.

[Conversation] This heading recounts actual conversations I have had. In some instances, they recount conversations I wish I had had. In any case, they are forums in which I can unapologetically address the reader and reminisce, offer advice, or report my biases.

[Definition] Definitions attempt to explain terminology and make abbreviations understandable.

[**Exercise**] Exercises are low-impact activities that I hope will illuminate a certain point or invite the reader to consider certain courses of action.

[**Joke**] I have been a life-long collector of jokes about information technology. Among my most important discoveries was the impact of humor—and the danger of telling jokes. What can I say? I like to live dangerously. If the reader prefers to avoid all risk of offense, let him overlook these items.

[**Quotation**] To qualify for inclusion here, a quotation must have passed at least two of three tests: Test one: "That's profound." Test two: "That's funny!" Test three: "That's relevant to the subject matter at hand." In the earnest hope that some quotations will be new to readers, each quotation is identified with some biographical information, including dates, of its author.

[**Speech**] I speak to a large number of groups, both managerial and technical. Though most of my speeches are forgettable, unpredictably I say something that warms the crowd. I offer a few samples here on the chance that what works from the podium will work also in print.

Techno Vision, then, is a tool for use by specific businesspeople for a specific, and usually serious, business purpose. It is intended to be read conventionally: starting at the beginning, where the problem addressed by the book is articulated and finishing at the end, where, it is hoped, some useful prescriptions are offered. But it has also evolved into a book in which to dip randomly. It has become a book for browsers. And though the subject of the disconnect between executives and information technologists is serious, with serious repercussions, there is plenty of scope for amusement. I have resisted few such opportunities for levity.

Introduction

From Computer Literacy to Information Literacy— Notes from an Informal Talk by Peter Drucker

As keynote speaker at the first CEO technology retreat sponsored by Computer Associates International and The CEO Institutes, America's pre-eminent management expert brought historical perspective to a problem that has been around for 100 years.

The first management conference of which we have any knowledge was called in 1882 by the German Post Office. The topic— and only chief executive officers were invited—was how not to be afraid of the telephone.

Nobody showed up. The invitees were insulted. That they as CEOs should use a telephone—this was unthinkable. The telephone was for underlings.

I was reminded of this story in the early sixties when I worked with IBM, on making the computer accessible to executives. Some of us then already understood that this wasn't just another gimmick but something that would profoundly, even fundamentally change the way we organize industry, the way we do business, that information would become the main productive factor. So IBM's Tom Watson, Jr. had a brilliant idea. We would have a meeting for CEOs and we would talk about "computer literacy." In fact, it was on that occasion that we coined the term.

However, I immediately tried to talk Tom Watson out of this brilliant idea by telling the story of the German Post Office. I said, "You're at that same stage—nobody's going to show up. It's too weird for them."

And, believe me, twenty-five or thirty years ago that kind of meeting was indeed not possible. And twenty years from now, it will not be necessary. Because twenty years from now you are going to be succeeded by the generation of my grandchildren.

If you know this generation, if any of you have children who are ten to thirteen years old, then you won't be surprised to hear what I learned from my own twelve-year-old grandson.

I was in Chicago two weeks ago visiting my youngest daughter and her children. My grandson, a very nice boy, is at twelve no longer into computers. That's kid stuff. He is now into soccer and skiing, but he keeps his hands in, you might say. He said, "Grandfather, Daddy's computer is no longer state-of-the art." What's the joke? My son-in-law happens to be a professor of physics and runs one of the biggest nonmilitary computer installations there is. But, as it happens, my grandson was right.

When this generation grows to adulthood and moves into your jobs we won't have to talk about computer literacy. Just as we no longer have to talk about how not to be afraid of the telephone. My grandson's five-year-old sister can dial the world over. And does. She doesn't have to be taught how not to be afraid of the telephone.

Of course it is not only my grandson who is computer literate. So is his whole generation in this country. This is one area where we are way ahead. Computer literacy is just beginning in Japan and it's still totally unheard of in Europe. My wife has nieces and nephews in Germany and their children know nothing, though as it happens the parents are both engineers. Oh yes, the parents work with computers but the idea that nine- or ten-year-olds should be familiar with computers is just beginning.

So we are way ahead on this one, but not quite where we should be. You yourselves are at this technology retreat because you have no doubt realized that, even though you have the top job in your company, you need to be computer literate. Otherwise your chief information people are going to make monkeys out of you. You have to be computer literate in self defense.

But believe me, ten or fifteen years hence, not only will we take computer literacy for granted, we will have had to learn how to be information literate.

And that, very few people are.

Most of you still believe that it is the job of the chief information officer to tell you what information you need. Would you now accept that this is a misunderstanding? Why? Because the information officer is a tool-maker. You are the tool-user.

Let me illustrate. Two weekends ago, I got to repairing that overstuffed sofa in our guest room that I should have repaired three years ago. So I went down to the hardware store to get the right kind of hammer, an upholstery hammer, and I asked the hardware store owner which hammer would be best for this task. He picked it out for me.

Now, I didn't ask him whether I should repair the sofa or not. Deciding that was my job. I merely asked him for the right tool. And he gave it to me. And when I had my fax machine installed two years ago, I had the telephone-installer come in to put in a new line and he was very helpful. He looked and said, "You may have chosen the wrong place to put it. I think it would be awkward over there. Why don't you put it here? And I can easily give you a line here too." But he didn't tell me to whom to send faxes or what to say in them. This is my job. His job was to give me the tool.

You must accept the fact that if the computer is a tool, it is the job of the tool-user to know what to use it for. So the first thing practically everyone must learn is to take information responsibility.

This means asking what information do I need to do my job, from whom, in what form, and when. And you're going to have to ask what information do I owe, to whom, in what form and when—not only so that others can do their jobs, but so that they can enable me to do my job. Unfortunately, most of us still expect the chief information officer or some other technologist to do that. It won't do.

I teach in a small graduate school. About 12 years ago we wanted to have a computer science building. When it came to raising the money we beat out Stanford and we beat out Yale and got an enormous amount of corporate money because we said in our proposal: "This school will not be in business in ten years. If we do a halfway decent job, it will have become superfluous. In ten years there will be computer engineers, there'll be people who design software, but computer science as a separate discipline in a management school will be gone. We got an enormous amount of money simply because we said that in ten or fifteen years we are not going to have to spend a great deal of time on creating the tool makers. We'll need them, of course. But we will have users who'll know how to use the tool, so that making the tool remains important, but purely technical.

To use the tool, the first step is to take information responsibility: What information do I need to do my job? In what form? Then the information specialists say, "Look, you can't get it in this form. You can get it in that form," well, that's relatively unimportant and relatively technical. It is the basic questions that are important: When do I need it, from whom so that I can do my job and, in turn, what information do I owe?

We are rebuilding organizations around information. When you talk of eliminating management levels you begin to use information as a structural element. Many times we discover very quickly that most levels of management—not many, most—do not manage anything.

They are simply relays to amplify those very faint signals that come down from the top and amplify the equally faint signals that come up from the bottom. I imagine all of you have heard of the first law of information theory that every relay doubles the noise and cuts the message in half. So do most management levels. They don't make decisions and don't manage anybody. They are only relays. When we build information in as a structural element we don't need them.

This creates enormous problems. For instance, where will the opportunities for promotion be tomorrow? Very few businesses will have more than two or three layers. Will you accept the fact that if you have more than three layers you are misorganized? You violate a basic rule: Very few people get into a management job before they are 26 or 27. You have to be in a job five years, not only to learn it, but to prove yourself in it. And yet, you have to be young enough to be considered for a senior management job before you're fifty. And that gives you three levels of management.

If you look at GM today versus yesterday, they've slimmed a little bit. They had 29 layers. Which means that nobody could really be considered for a top management job before age 211. This is part of the problem at GM.

So where will the promotion opportunities come from? How will we reward and recognize people? But also, how will we prepare people for jobs that are not functionally narrow?

These are very big challenges. And we don't know the answers, except for one thing: we will pay much more. Money will become far more important because in the past thirty years we have substituted title for money in many cases. We have had these rapid promotions in title with very little promotion in money. That's over.

Far more important is the change in the process. When we learn to use information as a tool, we are learning what to use it for, what we need, in what form, when, from whom and so on. The moment you examine these questions you realize that the information you need, the really important information, you cannot truly get from your information system. Your information system gives you inside information. But there are no results inside a business.

Many, many years ago I coined the term profit center. I am thoroughly ashamed of it. Because inside a business there are no profit centers. There are only cost centers. Profit comes only from the outside. When the customer returns with a repeat order and his check doesn't bounce, then you have a profit center. Until then you have only cost centers.

When we talk about the global economy, I hope you don't believe that you can possibly manage in it. Nobody can. There is no information on it.

But, if you are in the hospital field you can know hospitals. If you parachute down in some strange place and make your way to the lights in the valley, you will identify the correct building as a hospital. Even in Inner Mongolia, I can assure you that you will know that you are in a hospital. No mistaking it. No mistaking a school. No mistaking a restaurant.

People who tell me they operate in the world economy are those whose shares I sell immediately. One cannot operate where one can't know anything. We simply have no information at all. You can't know everything. You can only know what you know. This is why the enterprise of tomorrow is going to be very narrow in its focus.

Diversification can only work if you have the information. And you don't have it if the competition can come in from Osaka without any warning. We have so little information on the outside, on markets, on customers. Nothing, as some of you have learned the hard way, is changing faster than distribution channels. And if you wait until you get the report, it is way too late.

Technology itself is the perfect illustration. It's no longer the nineteenth century, or even the twentieth, where you could assume that the technologies that pertain to and affect your industry come out of your industry. Time has overthrown the idea behind the great research labs, of which the IBM lab is probably the last. There will be no other one like it. Most of what really had impact on the computer and the computer industry did not come out of IBM's own lab. Most of the brilliant things that came out of its lab IBM couldn't use in its own business. And that holds true of the Bell Labs, and of the pharmaceutical labs.

Technology is no longer a series of parallel streams which in the nineteenth century underlay our academic disciplines. It's a criss-cross, it's chaotic and therefore has to come from outside. And about this outside we don't know anything.

Here you are, a pharmaceutical manufacturer, and you are going to be made obsolete by mechanical instruments or proc-esses—say, by a pacemaker or a bypass. Most cardiac medicine has been. You may have the world's best lab, but the changes in your business will not come out of your lab. Your lab is focused on the inside, and so is our information system.

In effect, we are trying to fly on one wing, the wing of inside information. The big challenge will not be in getting more or better inside information, but how to add to that a little bit of outside information.

Let me give you an example. Most people believe this country has a balance-of-trade deficit. Most people are wrong, but don't know it. The balance-of-trade concept was developed around 1950, when a bright cookie had an idea. But this brilliant idea was limited to merchandise trade, and that is the only figure that is reported.

So this country today has a merchandise trade deficit but it happens to have an enormous service trade surplus. The official one is two-thirds of the merchandise trade deficit. The actual figure is probably much bigger because the real service trade figures are simply not there. For instance, we have 500,000 foreign students in this country; the minimum they bring in is $15,000 each. Therefore we have about $7 billion to $8 billion in foreign exchange income from these non-American students. And it is simply not reported.

I believe we actually may have a total merchandise and service surplus though only a very small one. The figures aren't there. Only the concept.

Our biggest challenge will continue to be getting this type of outside information to provide material for decision-making. This relates to the domestic market, the way customers are changing, the way distribution systems are changing, and it relates to technology and competition, because both can put you out of business. When the pacemaker hit, the market for the most profitable cardiac medicine disappeared in five years. It was only after the market had disappeared that these people said, "What happened?" So we need outside information, and we will have to learn, but it is complicated.

This is because you have two information systems in your business. One is organized around the data stream and the other one, which is far older, around the accounting system. The accounting system is an information system that is 500 years old and in terrible shape. The changes you will see in information technologies over the next 20 years are nothing compared to the changes you will see in accounting.

We have already begun to see changes in manufacturing cost-accounting, whose roots are in the 1920s and which is totally obsolete. But that is only for manufacturing, not service. Manufacturing today accounts for 23 percent of GNP and perhaps 16 percent of employment, which indicates that for the vast majority of business we have no accounting that's worth anything.

The problem with service business accounting is simple. Whether it's a department store or a university or a hospital, we know how much money comes in and we know how much money goes out. We even know where it goes. But we cannot relate expenditures to results. Nobody knows how.

Today these two systems are totally separate. They will not be for your children's generation. Your generation still depends on the accounting model. I don't know a single business yet which makes its decisions based on the data-processing stream. You all make decisions based on the accounting model and everybody in this room has learned from experience how easily this model may be manipulated. You know where you can trust it and where not. All of you have fallen through thin ice often enough not to walk on every part of it. You have learned to depend on cash flow because any accounting student in the second year of the course can manipulate any P&L. By the next generation, when the data-processing stream is more familiar, we will be able to merge the two or at least make them compatible. They are not compatible today. We teach them separately in the schools.

Likewise we have an accounting major and a computer science major and the two don't talk to each other: different concepts. Both departments are, as a rule, headed by people who know nothing about information. The person who heads up your accounting system knows government requirements. The head of data processing knows hardware. He or she doesn't know information.

We will have to bring the two together but we don't yet know how. My own guess is that 10 years from now a medium sized company, let alone a large one, will have two totally different people. It will have the chief financial officer, who will not manage anybody. His or her concern will be managing the corporation's money, and the biggest part of that will be managing foreign exchange. Tough enough now and soon to become much worse.

And it will have a chief information officer, who will be managing its information systems. The company will probably need both. They look at the world and the business quite differently.

But neither is yet focused on the wealth-producing capacity of the business. Neither is yet focused on tomorrow's decisions. They are both focused basically on what happened, not on what might happen or could be made to happen.

So we have an enormous job ahead of us. We are just beginning. Twenty-five years ago, if we had a meeting like this one today, you wouldn't have shown up. You would have been insulted. And even ten, fifteen years hence, your successors won't need it. But in the meantime, we will have to learn to make ourselves and our businesses information literate.

The job begins with the individual. The individual must become a tool-user. He or she must look at information as a tool for doing a specific job, which very few people yet do. Most of those who do are not in business. The people who have gone the furthest are in the military.

The second big job we have is to use our data-processing capacity to get the information we really need on what is happening on the outside. Here, what is available is usually in poor form and pretty unreliable. The only companies that have any information of this kind are the big Japanese trading houses. They have information about the outside—what they have about Brazil is amazing. But it took them 40 years and a great deal of money.

For most of you, the most important information is not about your customers, but about your noncustomers, because that's where the changes occur.

Look at what has become an endangered species, the American department store. Nobody had more information about its customers than the American department store. Until the eighties they held onto their customers. But they had no information about noncustomers. They had 28 percent of the retail market, the largest single share. However, this meant that 72 percent didn't buy at the department store. About these people the department stores had no information and couldn't have cared less. So it totally escaped them that the new customers, especially the affluent, do not shop in department stores. Nobody knows why. They don't. They are nondepartment store customers. By the end of the eighties, they had become the dominant customer group, determining the way all of us shop. Nobody in the department store world knew that because they had been looking at their own customers. After a time they knew more and more about less and less.

So we will have to organize information from the outside where the true profit centers are, and then we will have to build a system that gives this information to those who make the decisions. To do this we will have to bring together the accounting system and the data-processing system. Very few people have shown the slightest interest in doing this. We're at the beginning.

If you are not computer literate please do not expect anyone in your organization to have any respect for you. The young people in your businesses take it for granted; they expect at least literacy from the boss. My five-year-old granddaughter would have no respect if I said, "You know, I'm afraid of the telephone." She wouldn't even believe me. But my own grandfather was still afraid of the telephone.

Times change and we must change. We are at the point where we are beginning to move from computer literacy—basically knowing the ABCs, knowing the multiplication table or know-ing the four elementary arithmetic transactions—to doing some-thing with them. And that's going to be a very exciting and very, very challenging prospect for the years ahead.

We are just beginning to get into that stream. It's going to be a fast one.

Part 1
The Disconnect

Unlike historians, those of us living through a crisis lack the luxury of assigning clever names to disagreeable events. Years from now, the situation that I label "the disconnect" may well be known by a different term. The shorthand we use is irrelevant. The consequences we endure are not. By whatever designation, the disconnect that has evolved over the past 30 years between corporate executives and the managers of the information technology resource represents an enormous drain on the productivity and competitiveness of the United States. The disconnect has profound and sweeping implications for both you and your organization.

[Definition]

The Disconnect: A conflict, pervasive yet unnatural, that has misaligned the objectives of executive managers and technologists and that impairs or prevents organizations from obtaining a cost-effective return from their investment in information technology.

That this disconnect exists is hardly news. The promise of information technology seems almost infinite. Yet there is remarkable agreement that corporate America's investment in information technology has not delivered on its promises.

Few CEOs defend the record of information technology. Many have horror stories of lost revenues, failed initiatives, and missed opportunities. Despite investing billions of dollars in automating business processes, American business productivity has not risen to the promised levels. Entire industries first developed here have moved offshore. Organizations shed jobs in the same proportion that they lose market share to international competitors. These are just some of the consequences of the disconnect.

As far as I have been able to tell, no one has articulated the cause and scope of the disconnect or its consequences. As a result, the failures in information technology often appear as an indiscriminate avalanche of unrelated incidents, mostly having to do with hardware, software, and random technology events. The truth is much more complicated. The problem cannot be solved by better technology. Attractive as it may be to blame computers for the difficulties I have described, the fact is that we are talking about a longstanding management attitude. The fault is not, as Shakespeare might have observed, in the software, but in ourselves.

As long as we persist in thinking about the disconnect as a technology issue, we cannot begin to resolve it. Yes, many computer projects are never delivered, and those that are seem perennially late, overbudget, and full of bugs. Computer hardware can be so difficult to use as to be user-hostile. It is not surprising, then, that people have regarded the computer crisis in American business as a computer problem. If it is a computer problem, this argument logically follows, then it is appropriate that the folks in information technology should solve it.

But the disconnect has almost nothing to do with computers. It is a problem for the CEO. Nor can the problem be offloaded. I say the disconnect is the one senior management problem that the CEO cannot delegate. Moreover, just as the problem cannot be delegated away, it cannot be blamed away. As long as we blame technology—as long as we blame any one person or thing—we are powerless to combat the disconnect.

[Definition]

Information Technology (IT): A fundamental force in reshaping organizations by applying investments in computing and communications to promote competitive advantage, customer service, and other strategic benefits.

Information technology is not yet the largest industry in the world; it's just the most important. At $360 billion a year, computing runs well behind the petroleum and automobile industries. But because of its power to transform the way people work and think, the development of the computer has changed the world as much as the introduction of movable type and books. The microprocessor, only two decades after its invention, has turned everything we know about business inside out. In the process, it has obliterated hundreds of thousands of jobs, unseated some CEOs and made others wealthy, reshuffled millions of relationships, and set off convulsions that have left no organization untouched.

The $50 million Computer Associates I led in the early eighties is now an organization with revenues exceeding $2 billion. The problems of the disconnect have, if anything, kept pace with revenues. Information technology has emerged as the single most important discriminator between success and failure in the intensely competitive global economy. The lessons of information technology are critical not just to CEOs and CEO wannabees but to every participant in the enterprise. It is only the disconnect that creates an environment where this conclusion is not paramount.

Eliminating the disconnect encompasses fundamental change in just about everything having to do with the application of information technology. Yet the changes, by and large, will not be technological. It is not a question of building better computers or more reliable software. Nor will you need any skills you do not already have. By looking at the disconnect as a dysfunctional partnership between business and information technology managers, we can begin to take steps that confront the core issues and resolve them. Those steps require us to take an unflinching look at our own behaviors over the years and make corrections.

Any other approach will fail.

1
What on Earth Is Going on Here?

What is the frustration of CEOs over information technology? As chairman of the world's largest software company for business, I have met with hundreds of CEOs from companies around the world, many of whom seem to have a great deal in common when it comes to the subject of information technology. They invariably have a love/hate relationship with computers: CEOs love what they have been promised; they hate what they have been delivered. And they are frustrated as hell because they can't get straight answers to a simple question: Is this all we get for our money?

The frustration comes in many forms, but these are the four most common signals:

1. Despite their bewilderment by information technology, these CEOs are often proud of their investments in computers. In many cases, the computers represent the biggest single investment the company has or is likely to make. The stakes—both emotional and financial—are high.

2. Yet few CEOs are able to quantify the result. Unlike an investment in machine tools or real property, the yield from information technology seems to defy measure. Although many computer projects are duds, some projects turn out to be gleefully successful. This is crazy-making for many CEOs.

3. Economics aside, every company has teams of really smart and protective people dedicated to the care and feeding of these complex machines. As a result, many CEOs resign themselves to not understanding the technology. Instead, they find themselves dependent on a resident technologist— usually called a chief information officer or CIO.

[Definition]

CIO: Chief Information Officer, formerly the corporate data processing specialist. The title is used both specifically and generically.

---

4. For reasons the CEO often misunderstands, the partnership between the CEO and CIO is strained and not effective. Precisely because of this misunderstanding, the principals have been by and large powerless to make the partnership healthy.

It is the unproductive partnership between these two managers, the CEO and the CIO—so representative of the gulf between business and information technology—that is cause for most of the frustration over technology. But frustration should not be seen as the main byproduct of the disconnect—it is simply the most obvious symptom. The larger result of the disconnect between business and technology is often poor performance of information technology within the business.

But not always. Their frustration reaches critical mass precisely because a few computing projects succeed, some spectacularly so. I believe it is the *unpredictability* of information technology that drives most CEOs to distraction. No one seems to be able to predict with any confidence the outcome of individual information technology projects. Why are some projects immediate successes when most are late, overbudget, or, when finally delivered, massively irrelevant? After three decades of managing these projects, no one seems to have a clue.

CEOs must be aware that some companies have indeed remade themselves through information technology. Certain well publicized information technology initiatives offer CEOs the possibility of exceptional returns on investment. Gushing case histories about American Airlines' SABRE reservation system and Federal Express' GLOBEX package tracking system are required reading in every MBA program in the country. In practice, however, executives don't need an MBA to figure out that many computing projects fall considerably short of even modest goals.

This troubling paradox—why them, not me?—need not remain a mystery forever.

Companies that use information technology successfully are led by CEOs who have come to terms with information technology. They have not become information technology experts—the field changes too rapidly to allow that. They *have* decided to learn enough of the basic terminology and concepts to at least create a favorable climate for the introduction and deployment of information technology for the good of the organization.

These CEOs also refuse to look at information technology as a kind of corporate black hole, which sucks in money but whose effect can never be measured. Such CEOs are not afraid to ask simple questions. Nor are they afraid to appear ignorant. Rather, they familiarize themselves with the issues and insist on straightforward answers to questions such as:

- What business problem does the suggested project address?
- How is that better than what we have now?
- What is the ultimate cost?
- Does this estimate include retraining expenses—typically larger than the cost of the information technology installation itself— or will training costs be conveniently obscured in another department's budget?

- How reliable is the system—99 percent? What happens when the fateful 1 percent has its day?
- Is this new technology compatible with our old information technology investment?
- If not, is there an alternative that is?
- If so, what are the advantages of keeping our legacy system and upgrading it?
- In other words, how will this project help us be a more profitable bank, shoe manufacturer, airline, ad agency, retailer?

This is not brain surgery. It's Management 101. That millions can be spent before these questions are even asked is commonplace in a world that is both technology-dependent and technology-ignorant. Yet it need not continue if all parties to the development of the disconnect accept their mutual responsibility for eliminating it.

A growing number of CEOs, CIOs, and other managers have already taken steps to eliminate the disconnect. In ways large and small, these managers acknowledge the consequences to their businesses and America if the status quo is allowed to continue unchecked. Many of these champions of change—such as General Electric's Jack Welch—are celebrated for their ability to flatten the organization and effectively focus information technology resources. Most others work quietly for transformation, seeking consensus, learning technology, and persistently asking questions that are not universally regarded as career-advancing. If the disconnect is eliminated, it will be because of a critical mass of people like them.

The following chapters outline some steps that will assist these professionals. But before we consider specific steps, I think it is useful to consider how the disconnect developed over the past three decades.

[Quotation]

We've given you an unlimited budget and you've already exceeded it!   ANONYMOUS CEO

2
The Development of the Disconnect

The disciplines of executive management and information management have taken totally different evolutionary paths. Is it surprising, therefore, that the practitioners of each discipline have evolved unique cultures, values, and vocabularies even as they have attempted to coexist? The disconnect is based on the perpetuation and even glorification of these differences.

That the disconnect has been allowed—and sometimes encouraged—to persist defies reason. Until recently, some organizations have actually encouraged the creation and maintenance of a separate information technology subculture immune from the normal rules that govern the rest of the enterprise. These companies have developed unique policies, career ladders, and compensation plans for their computer workers. It would be as if an organization had a completely different set of standards and expectations for people in, say, Human Resources or Accounts Payable. By applying a set of career paths and incentives unique to information technology, organizations isolated the information technology function, ostensibly so that it could perform its mysterious tasks better. Most of these misguided efforts grew out of general technophobia and mistrust of computers.

In retrospect, it's not difficult to see why the information technology culture was so feared. Over the last three decades, computing and communications technologies have become increasingly critical components to successful business management. The community of technical professionals needed to support these information technologies grew out of a population that had their own set of values, assumptions, and jargon—all of which were quite unfamiliar to those from finance- or marketing-driven corporate management. Because of these differences, information technology and executive objectives have gradually diverged and the gap between them has grown.

The isolation of information technologists is the unintended consequence of the evolution of the data center in traditional organizations. In the 1950s, when mainframe computers were commercially introduced, organizations were appropriately concerned about the physical environment of these machines. Mainframes were large, expensive—they were among the largest capital expenses in their corporate owner's history—and mysterious. Companies were proud of their latest acquisitions and, like the art collector displaying rare, jeweled Fabergé eggs, were quick to build glass display cases where these machines could be periodically exhibited and then, for the remaining 364 days of the year, vaulted for safety.

Organizations erected these glass houses—so called because glass walls preserved the air-conditioned climate the sensitive machines required—to physically protect the data processing machines from threats environmental and human. But gradually the glass house and the values that developed within its hermetically sealed walls diverged from the culture of the organization whose mission it ostensibly supported. In some cases, the isolation of the data center was so complete that the prosperity of the organization was totally unlinked from the fortunes of information technology. In the most extreme cases, an attitude developed I can only describe as parasitic. In these extreme cases, the legitimate relationship between the data center and the organization was entirely reversed: The perception inside the glass house was that the organization existed to ensure the data center's continued survival.

It is no coincidence that the disconnect flowered at the same time one hardware vendor, IBM, overwhelmed the information technology market. Customers had few alternatives in the early days of proprietary mainframes. A dominant IBM helped maintain the disconnect because it benefited the vendor to keep both CEOs and technical managers passive and in the dark when it came to making information technology decisions. The proprietary account control system made customers so dependent on the primary hardware vendor that, for all intents and purposes, they forfeited meaningful choice. In more than a few data centers, incredibly, the hardware sales representative substantially determined the organization's information technology destiny. I remember visiting data centers where the IBM sales rep even had his own office.

My point is not to imply that IBM was alone in this practice. Every hardware vendor—Burroughs and Univac (now Unisys), Honeywell, NCR (acquired by AT&T), Control Data—used its proprietary lock-in to keep its customers dependent. Vendors kept a wedge between executive and technical management precisely to maintain the vendor's interests. This was known as *account control*. It was perceived to be in the vendor's interests, and the vendor, quite reasonably, perpetuated it! I don't fault any of the vendors for this practice. Had I been the CEO of any of them, it is probably what I would have done.

The overpowering influence of the hardware vendors contributed to the disconnect in a number of ways. Most of all, it helped keep people stupid. The most benign interpretation of account control is that, to the extent IBM played a reasonable enabling role, it relieved many executives and information technology managers of their responsibility to be informed. It also, not coincidentally, robbed them of the opportunity to work together for the unalloyed good of the organization. A less charitable view is that account control was a massive conspiracy against computer users, a case that the Antitrust Division of the Justice Department labored mightily to make.

Account control was a symptom of the disconnect. Over the years, account control made computing hundreds of billions of dollars more expensive than it needed to be. These resources could have been put to work developing new products, introducing innovative services, and building stockholder value for a large number of organizations instead of enriching a small number of hardware vendors.

The good news is that account control is dead. The competitive world of commodity computing killed it. In the open systems world, customers can exercise much wider freedom of choice in their hardware and software vendors. This freedom of choice, customers find, represents opportunities for significant savings. Hardware and software vendors must now find other ways of winning customer loyalty.

Ironically, as the disconnect eases in this particular area and freedom of choice replaces account control, hardware and software suppliers are transforming the vendor-customer relationship into a strategic partner relationship. Customers recognize the value of freedom of choice and will exercise it if a partner screws up, but most customers prefer dealing with a small number of loyal strategic partners. Stable relationships are in everyone's interests. The difference is that the open market optimally aligns the interests of the strategic partners and doesn't favor one over the other.

[Quotation]

Twenty, 30 years ago, people didn't have to be technologists because the vendors backed up a dump truck to the data center door and unloaded it. They told you when the next upgrade was coming and you took it.

WARREN L. HARKNESS
Director of Information Services,
Bose Corp., Framingham, Massachusetts

Many CEOs believed they were being respectful of information technology when they agreed to a different set of standards for information technology, tossed accountability out the window, and threw up their hands at a situation perceived to be unmanageable. They could not have been more short-sighted. Among all others, this attitude of detachment most accounts for the deplorable situation that developed. The attitude, unfortunately, is not completely unknown even today.

CEOs actually joked about how unmanageable the situation was. Referred to as software nerds, computer jockeys, or bit heads, information technology workers were perceived to be essentially out of control. Business people snickered at programmers with their white socks and shirt pocket protectors filled with colored pencils. Underneath this teasing was a conviction, often grounded in some reality, that executives didn't have the first clue about how to manage programmers and other technical professionals. Ultimately, this attitude equaled nothing less than giving up.

The truth was that many executives felt uncomfortable with their information technology people because the executives were uncomfortable with technology itself. After struggling to make sense of the situation, many CEOs quickly grew frustrated and literally left the computer people to their own devices or, in exasperation, assigned management of information technology to the CFO, hoping that he or she could at least keep the costs down. Predictably, the easiest thing to do was for corporate executives to avoid the people in information technology. To justify this practice, they rationalized that information technology either worked better without management, didn't need management, or was impossible to manage. (Pick one.)

Isolating information technology and regarding it with a mix of fear and mystery was supposed to be evidence of the supreme importance in which information technology was regarded. In truth it had the opposite effect. By isolating information systems from the fabric of the business, information technology became marginalized and the objectives of the technologists diverged even more from the objectives of the business leaders. By the mid-1960s, the disconnect was in full bloom.

If the disconnect formed so early, why is it only now that we are feeling the pain?

The disconnect has always taken a toll on the health and wealth of organizations, but it has only been recently that the damage has been obvious. Still, American business has lived with the disconnect for three decades. What has transpired to turn a simmering evolutionary accident into a threat that, unless corrected, will boil American business alive?

Two major forces explain why the disconnect is suddenly so inescapable. First, information technology has only recently emerged as an enabler of strategic applications which single-handedly can determine a company's competitive edge. Thus the stakes have increased, as have the costs of failure. Second, global competition has unleveled the playing field. If every player in a game is hobbled by a similar disability, it's easy to overlook the common handicap. But the recent emergence of global competitors that by and large have avoided the disconnect makes the handicap impossible to ignore. Let us look at each of these forces in a little more detail.

Information Technology as an Enabler of Strategic Applications

In the dawn of the information technology era, the divergence of business needs and information technology resources was obscured by the limited role computers played and by the general prosperity of business in the 1950s and 1960s. Organizations had only one computer and its role was limited to back-room functions such as accounting and payroll. It was literally out of sight and out of mind.

When computing was limited to the back office, it was easy for executives to ignore computer problems. For many years, data centers served as black boxes into which a corporate department, such as the warehouse or accounts payable, would file a request for a computer application and later (sometimes years later) the black box would open and deliver a system. With a little luck, the system would be reminiscent of the application the department originally requested. More likely, it would be some anonymous system analyst's approximation of what the department wanted. Argument was futile because there was no appeal to the data center's conviction that it knew what users wanted better than the users themselves. In any case, the point was often moot because the passage of time had so altered the requesting workgroup's requirements that the original request was no longer relevant.

People were in less of a hurry, competition was less intense. And, since the organization had no clue as to how much information technology was actually costing, it was logical to deal with issues that were easier to measure. Why sweat it when everyone was prospering? American business flourished in the 1960s. There was enough to go around without justifying every little expenditure. Besides, every corporation had more or less the same problem, so everyone was penalized more or less evenly.

At the same time, senior executives became more isolated from the operational details of their companies. Corporations cultivated large bureaucracies of middle managers. Top executives began using middle managers as cops, protecting themselves from information technology and other unruly issues of the corporation. Middle managers learned that power stemmed from hoarding information, not sharing it. They became gatekeepers of information between senior executives and information technology, filtering directives on the way down and analyzing information on the way up. These filters perpetuated the disconnect by obscuring from senior management just how much of a rat's nest the information technology situation resembled.

Every bureaucracy breeds hesitation and absurdity. Like any bureaucracy, middle management had as its first agenda the duty to survive. The disconnected status quo was perfect for this purpose. Middle managers appreciated the disconnect and refined it by institutionalizing the disconnect as a valued aspect of corporate culture. If it was rare for a CEO to become partners with the information technology manager, it now became all but impossible. Going though channels became the order of the day and guess who controlled the channels? If middle management had not discovered the disconnect, it would surely have created it. And now, as downsizing disintegrates the layers of middle management, the disconnect becomes even more visible.

Four other issues conspired to raise the level of frustration to the breaking point:

1. Competition for information technology resources
2. Time compression related to market forces
3. Decentralization
4. Downsizing

These forces raised the stakes to an alarming level, making the costs of the disconnect impossible to ignore.

Competition. As demand for computer applications increased, competition for finite information technology resources became first intense, then ridiculous. Application backlogs—the waiting time users had to endure before their applications were even considered—often exceeded two years. User departments, fighting for attention and priority, became curious about the management practices within information technology. Complaints were so loud and relentless that senior management had no choice but to peel off the covers and take a look. Rarely was it a pretty sight. Prince Otto von Bismark warned that one should decline invitations to observe firsthand the construction of sausages and laws; he could have added to that list the development of information systems applications.

Time Compression. Business conditions became so volatile that waiting two years or more for an application was a luxury users could no longer afford. Having automated all their back room operations, companies had begun to computerize the strategic applications that leveraged emerging business opportunities. These systems could not wait. Forget next year; users needed their systems next week. The window of opportunity was too narrow to allow business as usual in the data center.

Decentralization. By the late 1980s, centralization as an organizing structure was no longer in favor. Decentralization, the third force putting pressure on the data center, encouraged customer-service-oriented companies to move resources closer to the customers being served. Although they resisted mightily, data processing departments were not spared. Like the fabled walls of Jericho, the glass walls came tumbling down in response to the raised voices of millions of frustrated users. Though centralized facilities continued to grow, many new computer resources were redeployed in factories, warehouses, departments, and workgroups spread throughout the organization. The disconnect that had for so long been quarantined by centralization was suddenly exposed for everyone to see.

It was during this time that people became aware of the lean and mean decentralized organizations that achieved excellence through alignment of their business objectives and decentralized, highly responsive information processing units. These groups raised the standards for delivering products and services. They were less hierarchical and therefore quicker. They were flattened and demassified and therefore cheaper. And they were empowered to customize products and services and therefore they won the hearts of customers. These decentralized organizations, most recently known as virtual organizations, raised the bar for their competitors. Good enough became not nearly good enough anymore.

Downsizing. The hierarchical structures organizations evolved in the 1950s, like the disconnect itself, can no longer be sustained. A number of forces, including global competition and information technology, have made downsizing inevitable.

Every day, it seems, headlines are filled with news about companies eliminating positions. That this downsizing is healthy on a macroeconomic level does not lessen the considerable pain and disruption it causes on the lives of individuals. But downsizing focuses much needed attention on how people and processes add value to the enterprise. Downsizing encourages organizations to think about meeting customer needs using small workgroups. And it compels organizations to ensure that information technology is aligned with the goals of these workgroups.

Global Competition Made the Playing Field Unlevel

For many years American companies dominated the business landscape. In 1960, *Fortune Magazine* listed the largest industrial corporations in the world. Eight of the companies were headquartered in the United States. This is what the list looked like:

Rank	Company name	Country	1960 sales ($ billion)
1.	General Motors	United States	12.736
2.	Standard Oil of New Jersey	United States	8.034
3.	Royal Dutch/Shell	Netherlands	5.481
4.	Ford Motor Company	United States	5.237
5.	General Electric	United States	4.197
6.	Unilever Bros.	Netherlands	3.883
7.	U.S. Steel	United States	3.698
8.	Socony Mobil	United States	3.178
9.	Chrysler	United States	3.007
10.	Texaco	United States	2.980

In 1992, the last year for which figures are available, the same list looked like this:

Rank	Company name	Country	1992 sales ($ billion)
1.	General Motors	United States	132.774
2.	EXXON	United States	103.547
3.	Ford Motor Company	United States	100.785
4.	Royal Dutch Shell Group	Netherlands	98.935
5.	Toyota Motor	Japan	79.114
6.	IRI	Italy	67.547
7.	IBM	United States	65.096
8.	Daimler-Benz	Germany	63.339
9.	General Electric	United States	62.202
10.	Hitachi	Japan	61.465

The three decades between 1960 and 1990 rocked the world. The United States changed from a net exporting country to a net importing country. It no longer dominates the list of largest companies of the world in any category. A comparison of every other category of business—transportation, financial institutions, food, semiconductors—shows the same reduction in American dominance. Even the few familiar names remaining on the list mask the reality. While General Motors remains the largest corporation in the world, it was also the biggest money loser, at $23.5 billion for 1992 alone.

Relentless competition has reduced key industries such as steel and automobiles to shadows of their former selves. Entire industries pioneered in the United States have been allowed to march offshore. Television and video cassette recorders (VCRs), both invented and developed in the United States, are no longer even manufactured in the United States. I am not suggesting that all of America's economic problems in the last three decades can be attributed to the disconnect between management and information technology. But many of America's economic woes must be laid squarely at the door of the disconnected corporation.

Did No One See the Danger?

Many far-sighted people over the years predicted the disconnect. Ever since the beginning of the Information Age, there have been isolated voices begrudging information technology's insatiable appetite for resources. These individuals correctly anticipated a runaway expense against the bottom line, but they were hobbled from demonstrating their case to senior managers because they lacked the tools and methods to measure exactly how much information technology was actually costing. Not surprisingly, information technology had failed to build auditing tools to monitor its activities in terms that corporate executives could understand. Since there was no way to measure the impact information technology imposed on the corporation's resources, managers predictably attended to matters that could be more precisely calibrated.

By the late 1960s, auditing firms for the Fortune 500 such as Arthur Young and Ernst & Whinney (now Ernst & Young) began to insist that the data processing function be made more accountable and auditable. These firms, recognizing the unprecedented role of information technology in the corporation, raised persistent questions about the integrity, security, and auditability of the corporate data maintained by the information technology resource. These questions—often posed to boards of directors for the first time—initiated some high-level inquiries.

During the same period, the attitude of "bigger is better" came under close scrutiny. This cultural change challenged the concept of large, consolidated data centers that required a centralized data processing function for its management. Forward-thinking corporate managers began to be troubled by these isolated departments dominated by people with unimpeachable technical skills but frequently limited management experience and occasionally massive indifference to overall corporate strategies and objectives. By the late 1970s, some of these data centers were perceived to be barriers to the departments they were supposed to serve.

When the glass houses were augmented by decentralized computing, the disconnect went away, right? Wrong. While American businesses moved resources around and certainly improved efficiency and accountability, they failed to address the root causes of the disconnect: Information technology artifacts were physically manipulated in a choreography of decentralization, but the root causes of the disconnect were not challenged.

[Quotation]

The factory of the future will have only two employees: a man and a dog. The man will be there to feed the dog. The dog will be there to keep the man from touching the computer.

WARREN G. BENNIS
American education and business writer, 1925–

3

What We Have Here Is a Failure to Communicate

Information technology has always been overmanaged but underdirected. This fact by itself accounts for at least 80 percent of the problems I'm defining as the disconnect.

Many CEOs acknowledge that they have not always carefully communicated strategic business objectives. Many have neglected to consult their information technology staffs until well after they have formulated such strategies. Others have been unwilling to acknowledge that information technology occupies a central role in fulfilling these objectives—or that a growing number of technical executives want to operate with the big picture in mind.

For their part, many technical executives have not developed the business and communication skills that would enable them to communicate more effectively with CEOs. While acknowledging their limitations, these technical executives have pleaded for an enlightened attitude among CEOs and a place at the strategic planning table. There they could gain the insight necessary to answer the fundamental question for information technology (or any department, for that matter): What business are we in and what can we do to maximize our value to that business?

[Dialogue]

CIO: You know, it's at times like this, when I'm six months behind on the project with no clue what to do and the company depending on me, that I really wish I'd listened to what my father told me when I was young.

CEO: Why? What did he tell you?

CIO: Excuse me. Did you say something? I wasn't listening.

One classic indication that information technology is too self-centered and is not supporting the company's business objectives is the users' perception that information technology is acting as an obstructionist, rather than as an assistant. Information technology must acknowledge what users want, not just give them what information technology believes they need. This means responding to user requests with choices rather than restrictions. Even when user requests are not feasible, information technology must provide alternatives and solutions instead of reasons, however technologically astute, why the requested project is not feasible.

[Speech to CEOs]

There's Enough Blame to Go Around

If CEOs stay at their average level of ignorance about information technology, they are doomed to failure.

Why expect your CIO to understand your business—or even business as a concept—when you yourself have reached maturity and never bothered to understand the simplest aspects of technology? If blame must be assigned, it might be best shared.

When you hired your CIO, did you ask how information technology improved profitability at the CIO's last workplace? Did you ask if the CIO identifies as a technologist or a businessperson? Did you inform the CIO that his or her principal responsibility would be to the bottom line, or did you merely murmur in assent when he or she talked about great changes, the technological cutting edge?

Did you ever ask if the candidate had ever taken a new assignment and reported that everything looked in order and nothing be changed?

Don't be surprised if few CIO candidates are able to admit to accepting the status quo. "Revolution" is the constantly uttered byword of information technology. There is, of course, a place for revolutionary products. But the thoughtful CEO must ask whether this company at this time is that place. To reach that point, the CEO must come to terms with technology, must learn the rudiments of the language, and must choose the CIO as he or she would any other member of the executive team. In doing so, the CEO might find that the CIO is happy to be part of a corporation that values his or her contribution to the income statement.

[Anecdote]

PC Potemkin Village

One of CA's regional sales managers recounted an experience that still makes me shake my head in knowing disbelief.

It was in the late eighties when he was closing a major sale at a large consumer products organization in the Midwest. The group concluding the negotiations was invited to the office of the CEO of the company. The sales manager was amazed to see a glittering, state-of-the-art PC on the polished teak credenza behind the desk of the executive. The salesman was duly impressed, not only by the fact that the executive had a PC but that it was such a powerful model.

At a moment when the others were busy reviewing a document elsewhere in the large office, the sales manager peeked behind the credenza. He was looking for the presence of a coaxial cable going into the wall. He wanted to know if the system was networked or simply a standalone PC. But what he saw amazed him and told him a lot about the organization. The computer of the CEO of a $5 billion company was devoid of a single cable. It wasn't even plugged in. Completely inoperative, the system was for show only.

What are the most common complaints CEOs have about CIOs? What are the most common criticisms CIOs whisper about CEOs? I decided to see if I could answer these questions. Using an informal, decidedly unscientific approach, I simply put the question to the next 200 CEOs and CIOs I spoke to. There were just two conditions. First, I asked the executives to be specific in their criticism. "Oh, he just doesn't understand!" is not criticism; it's blame. I have no use for blame. Second, I promised anonymity. After a full year of questioning, I have come up with the following short list of the most common symptoms of the disconnect.

First, let's look at the complaints CEOs make about CIOs. The CEOs had little use for CIOs who:

- Communicate in technical terms instead of business terms.
- Lose sight of the business when dealing with technological decisions.
- Remain ignorant of the company's customers and their needs.
- Fail to protect the CEO from information technology vendors.
- Don't keep key systems operational.
- Harbor judgments that nontechnical people, such as most CEOs, are pitiful.

Next, let's consider what complaints CIOs have about their CEOs. The CIOs had little use for CEOs who:

- Are not comfortable sharing strategic objectives.
- Resist having the CIO as a direct report.

- Refuse to explore how computer technology could help solve business problems.
- Persist in thinking of information technology only for automating accounting functions.
- Neglect to consider technology managers for added business responsibilities.
- Treat information technology professionals as less than equals.
- Are too insecure to ask technical questions for fear of appearing ignorant.
- Are not prepared to consider as peers their colleagues who manage information technology.

[Conversation]

The View from the Top: Five Tips for CIOs

I know of a number of organizations in which the CEOs and CIOs have the kind of cooperative partnership I've been describing. I have asked the CEOs at these progressive companies to list five behaviors and attitudes CIOs can practice to help build the kinds of disciplines that will most profit the enterprise.

1. *Keep your eyes on the business,* especially when dealing with complex and at times far-out technical decisions.

2. *No surprises.* What CEOs hate most is being blindsided by a problem or development. Keep the CEO apprised of all storms on the horizon, even if they are currently minor gusts.

3. *Just say no* to being the chief computer nerd in your company. Being the chief techie in an organization had a certain panache in the seventies, but in the nineties it's a one-way path to nowhere. CEOs welcome CIOs who ask for additional responsibility to demonstrate business management skills.

4. *Work your plan*. This old standby procedure is critical for complex technology projects on which companies stake their survival.

5. *Manage*. CEOs don't expect CIOs to have all the technical answers. They do expect them to have the project management experience to bring in projects on time and on budget.

[Quotation]

Having lost sight of our goal, we must redouble our efforts.

ANONYMOUS

[Exercise]

Information Technology from Scratch

Assume that the computer revolution never occurred and it's your thankless job to design from scratch a computer system to automate America's businesses. In a subversive funk, you decide to create the most frustrating and expensive system possible. Your design specifications are:

- Avoid, at all costs, any semblance of standardization. Instead, fragment the industry by rewarding participants to divide and conquer.

- Create and isolate a subculture of technicians divorced from the give and take of normal business. Evolve technical language full of jargon, buzzwords, and arcane acronyms.

- Create a computer supplier so dominant that most consumers become heavily dependent on that supplier.

- Endow the automation group with certainty that they know the organization's automation requirements better than the people actually using the automation.

- Build into the development process sufficient complexity and inertia to ensure that delivered systems are either late or substantially incomplete, preferably both.

Now, how is the hapless system you have designed distinguishable from the situation that has actually evolved?

[Joke]

What You See Is What You Get

A salesman plunked down two suitcases in front of an executive on a commuter train and said, "Sir, I think you might be interested in a very special watch I happen to be selling." The man shook his head firmly, "Beat it. I already have a watch."

"Ah, but you don't know what this watch can do," the salesman pointed out enthusiastically.

"Listen." He pushed a little button and a voice said clearly, "The time is six fifty-seven."

"Nice, but I don't need a watch."

"I quite understand, but just take a look at this." The salesman pushed another little button, and the dial turned into a tiny color television screen on which the evening news was coming through loud and clear.

"Impressive," admitted the executive, "but I already have a television."

"How about a Walkman?" The salesman unfolded little earphones from the watch strap, tuned the watch to a classical station, and watched the man as he listened to a passage from a Mozart concerto. Shaking his head, the executive put the watch on one of the large suitcases. "Sorry, no."

"But that's not all," the salesman continued, undeterred. "What's your home number?" He punched it into a tiny keypad, handed over the watch, and the man found himself speaking to his son over a perfectly clear connection.

Now, the executive was impressed. "Okay, how much?"

"Now there's the good news. You get a watch, a color television, a portable radio, and a cellular phone—all for only one eighty-nine ninety-five."

"All right," the executive said. "I'll take one."

Taking the executive's money, the salesman shook his hand, assured him he'd made a wise choice, and headed down the aisle.

"Wait!" the executive called out. "You forgot your sample cases!"

"Those aren't sample cases," the salesman called back. "They're the batteries."

4

Misinformation, Mythmakers, and Mayhem

Executives and technology managers didn't get into the miserable, disconnected situation by accident. No, we had considerable assistance from a group of mostly well-meaning people who, for a variety of predictable reasons, perceived it to be in their interests to leave a robust measure of confusion, complexity, and antagonism in their wake.

Every participant in the computer industry has, to one degree or another, been snookered or exploited by the forces I call the *ignorance lobby*. On the short list of the ignorance lobbyists are selected industry and management consultants and analysts, technology associations, and members of the media. I emphasize the word "selected." Consultants, analysts, associations, and journalists all make legitimate contributions to the computer industry. Indeed, it's hard to imagine an industry without them. Some of the industry's outstanding achievements can be traced to their efforts. Nevertheless, it's advantageous to consider their motives and agendas. Prudence dictates that if we are to counteract the effects of the excesses of the ignorance lobby, we must be acquainted with the forces that influence them.

Understanding just two fundamental principles puts the situation into perspective. The first principle is:

> *Many members of the ignorance lobby have a stake in your continued ignorance.*

Given this attitude, there is surprisingly little percentage in making things look easy. The more mystical and esoteric the ignorance lobby can make the situation, the more likely they are to command high fees, get subsequent assignments, raise association dues, or sell more advertising space. The second principle is even simpler:

> *Follow the money.*

If you can establish the financial incentives that members of the ignorance lobby have evolved, you are in a much better position to make appropriate discounts for their advice, counsel, and services. Now, everyone is entitled to compensation for services and expertise. Some of the best money I have ever spent went to consultants and analysts. But when I buy advice, I want that advice aligned with my objectives, not anyone else's. Analysts or consultants that are beholden to other parties, especially when I am not aware of those interests, serve no one but themselves. When that happens, even the soundest advice loses credibility.

A common characteristic of many of these groups is that they welcome upheaval. Change makes their jobs easier; in fact, change in many cases is just about the only thing that justifies their existence. Fortunately for the ones with integrity, the computer industry offers sufficient naturally occurring upheaval to gainfully employ an army of consultants, analysts, technical associations, and journalists. Unfortunately, some groups and individuals go out of their way to encourage an entirely artificial and unnecessary threshold of upheaval and confusion.

These are the *mythmakers*. Like the gods on Mount Olympus who were always vying for human subservience and devotion, the mythmakers offer pronouncements and edicts that inspire friction. Hired by organizations to resolve tension in the industry and promote consensus, they frequently do just the opposite. On principle, they make war on the status quo. They want to destroy the old in order for the new to succeed. Friction is useful for those who make a living by promoting change for the sake of change. Let's take a closer look at the groups that make up the ignorance lobby.

[Speech to CEOs]

Our Special Today: Technology-du-Jour

With the predictability of church bells on Sunday morning, the promise of new technology is heard in the corporation. Out with the old (and the old-fashioned), in with the new (and the newfangled). Sweeping change is called for. Oddly, the change turns out to be what some current technology experts are touting this year, this month, even this week.

Never mind that today's solutions keep changing or that some of these solutions have never yet solved anything at all. They have been recommended by a group of experts who have managed to make the most noise. They promote revolution.

The revolutionaries may be consultants. They may be editors of technology journals. They may actually represent the very companies that have a considerable financial stake in revolution. Acting together, they form an effective lobby for the new, the dramatically different—and the totally untested.

New technology usually means extensive and expensive retraining of staff, and much downtime. Downtime is hardly an abstraction. It is what happens when the person on the other end of the phone tells you the order cannot be processed because the computer is down. The result is a lost order, if not a lost customer. Downtime means loss. When the central customer service computer of the mail order company, Lands End, goes down, the company loses up to $1 million per hour.

Regardless of such hazards, the prevailing culture of business technology dictates the revolutionary approach. The current revolutionary war cry is, "Downsize!" This simply means replacing mainframes with smaller computers that are linked together. What is rarely said is that while this downsizing trend continues, the need for mainframe technology continues to grow. Many organizations continue to rely on their mainframe systems for their most demanding mission-critical computing. Vendors have responded with mainframe systems that are far more powerful and efficient than ever.

But all this hardly matters, because what is important to many experts is revolutionary change itself. If change were orderly, carefully staged, and evolutionary, there would hardly be any need for the revolutionaries.

Faced with what often amounts to technology-du-jour, and against the background of a bewildering array of technology, all labeled in precise Technobabble, CEOs are likely to depend excessively on their CIOs. Most CEOs are well acquainted with finance, operations, and other business issues. Many have had hands-on experience in these fields for many years. Some companies actually groom potential CEOs for the role by having them serve apprenticeships in Sales, Finance, Production, and Marketing. But how many CEOs have been cross-trained in information technology?

Not many. This is one source of the disconnect. So few CEOs are comfortable with even the simplest personal computers—the kind that their own children use so effortlessly at home—that the normative response is to call in an expert, ask for his or her opinion, authorize the check, and hold their breath. Well, holding your breath—or, in some cases, holding your nose—is not management.

Consultants and Analysts

We look to consultants and analysts for independent sources of expertise and advice. Independent analysts and consultants play a vital role because technology is changing so rapidly. As witnesses to many different approaches to a large number of problems, consultants and analysts are in a unique position to render judgments about the relative merits of these approaches.

Yet truly independent consultants are hard to find. Many consultants have a range of business relationships with hardware and software vendors. Some of these relationships are perfectly legitimate and aboveboard; others are less so. Downsizing creates a growing population of consultants who may be as independent as their search for a new employer.

Many books have been written on selecting and managing consultants, and it is not my goal to repeat this material. My point is that a small number of very vocal consultants and analysts play a prominent role in the proliferation of misinformation, myths, and mayhem in the computer industry. It's quite simply in their interests to do so; for as long as there are disputes there will be need of individuals to study, debate, and present those disputes. I have just one piece of advice about consultants and analysts:

It is better to be wrong than biased.

The most important attribute of a consultant or analyst is independence. If you don't have that, you are not dealing with a consultant at all, but a member of a profession considerably older. It reminds me of an old expression: A person who has but one watch knows what time it is; a person with two watches is never sure.

[Joke]

Here, Little Bird, Let Me Help You

A small bird lay freezing to death along a country lane in the Northern steppes. A peasant came along, saw the dying bird, and thought to himself, "If only I had something—anything—in which to wrap this bird, I might save its life." But, alas, he had nothing that he could spare in the face of the cold Russian winter. But then he saw some cow droppings nearby and he thought in desperation, "Perhaps if I wrap up the bird in that, it will warm the poor bird enough to save its life." He picked up the bird, wrapped it in the cow manure, laid it gently on the ground, and went on his way. Sure enough, the dung began to warm the bird. And it started to come to life again. The bird was so overjoyed at feeling warm again that it tried to sing. But all it could do in its weakened condition was some low, feeble notes.

Just then another peasant came along. He heard the bird's attempt at singing and thought, "Poor bird, it's choking in the cow dung." So he picked it up, removed the dung, and laid the bird back on the ground. Shortly thereafter, the bird froze to death.

There are three morals to the story.

- First, it isn't necessarily your enemies who put you in it.

- Second, it isn't necessarily your friends who get you out of it.

- And third, when you're in it up to here, for heaven's sake, don't sing.

The Computer Industry Media

The media reporting on the computer industry generally do a remarkable job of covering a fast-paced, increasingly important sector of the economy. Trade industry publications, technical newsletters, and general business magazines all offer news, analysis, product reviews, vendor ratings, and personality updates. But the disconnect is alive and well in the computer industry media because perpetuating it serves the interests of reporters, editors, and publishers. Without the ability to recognize how the disconnect biases reporting, CEOs and other executives will have a difficult time understanding the real issues.

Again, the problem is not accuracy, but bias. Many journalists are encumbered with two raging forces: their publishers and an instinct for controversy. It's not clear which force is more destructive to judicious journalistic coverage of the issues that are of the most benefit to men and woman working to address today's information technology challenges.

[Quotation]

Newspapers are unable, seemingly, to discriminate between a bicycle accident and the collapse of civilization.

GEORGE BERNARD SHAW
Irish dramatist, 1856–1950

Publishers are in the business of producing magazines and newspapers, right? Wrong. Their business is selling advertising space. To that end most publishers put out genuinely useful publications that deliver accurate information to their readers and provided targeted, interested readers to their advertisers. This is the contract and it's a sound one. Most publishers enforce a clear separation between the editorial and advertising departments so that no one can accuse them of covering or favoring vendor companies in return for advertising dollars. While the wall between editorial and advertising stands firm, subscribers can have confidence that editorial decisions are being made with their requirements and issues in mind. When the wall is breached, everyone loses.

When that happens, publishers abdicate an important role they could be playing in the industry. They could offer an independent voice on behalf of their readers, keeping the vendors, analysts, and other self-serving groups honest. But there is little percentage in offending a potential advertiser. So publishers sometimes serve as accomplices to the voices of friction, unwittingly offering their pages to more hype and hokum.

Computer journalists, like all reporters, have the sentiments of Hollywood script writers: They gravitate to drama and conflict, two qualities not naturally overabundant in the computer industry. Not to worry. If genuine conflict and discord is not forthcoming, it can be produced. And what's the perfect metaphor for conflict? You guessed it: a war. That's one of the driving forces behind the language wars, the database wars, the platform wars, and all the other mythical "wars" that are mostly sound and fury, signifying nothing. My point is this: Appreciate the underlying motivations of the media. Fierce competitive pressures, both economic and personal, encourage news coverage that is provocative and controversial. In war, truth is the first casualty. This is no less the case in the database wars, language wars, and platform wars that periodically entertain the industry.

In short, remember the old credo cigar-chomping city editors used to growl to cub reporters:

Believe nothing. If your mother says she loves you, check it out.

[Joke]

Vendor-Speak-to-English Dictionary

Do you ever get the impression that vendors sometimes say one thing but mean another? Ever wish you could get on-the-spot interpretation of what the vendor actually meant to say? Here is a quick reference guide for the systems shopper.

When they say this:	*They really mean this:*
Completely open.	There's a 50-percent chance that it will work with your existing systems.
Installed at over 250 sites.	Actively used by 25 sites, uninstalled at 25 sites, and 200 sites have filled out bingo card requesting information.
Complete interoperability among standard computing platforms.	We'll do Windows and UNIX first, and you can hold your breath waiting for the OS/2 and Macintosh versions.
Twenty-four-hour hotline support.	It'll take us at least 24 hours to get back to you.

Announcing a completely new architecture customizable to your specific requirements.	Architecture announcements we have out the wazoo; just don't pin us down on delivery.
Our customers have the benefit of scalability.	Watch as we try to sell you bigger and bigger machines.
We deliver support for industry-standard application programming interfaces.	We couldn't figure out any other way to make this product operate with any other vendor's product.
We operate in a fully heterogeneous environment.	If our product doesn't work, we can always blame the other vendors.
Fully object-oriented at the physical and logical levels.	Our only object is to get payment. Good luck on finding the logic.

5

The FUDGE Factor

Another set of issues clouds the thankless but necessary process of acquiring computer hardware. The whole process of technology acquisition is blurred by a set of attitudes I call the FUDGE factor.

The term "FUD" is certainly not new. It's a longstanding computer industry term (circa 1960), coined by IBM's competitors who were frustrated by Big Blue's early dominance of the computer industry. *FUD* stands for Fear, Uncertainty, and Doubt. To organizations whose fortunes were inexorably linked to IBM's product announcements, the term "FUD" penetrated to a palpable anxiety that they would be left behind. IBM salespeople used "FUD" as their theme song and played it like virtuosos. I personally witnessed the following variations on a theme:

- *The Fear:* "Sure Amdahl Corporation's storage devices are cheaper than IBM's, but where will you be if, by chance, next year we stop supporting them?"

- *The Uncertainty:* "Now I can't be sure when, but support for system X will be frozen. However, if you upgrade now ..."

- *The Doubt:* "Let's say for the sake of argument that Computer Associates' database management system is more efficient than ours. Can you be sure that they'll be around in 10 years?"

People have lived with "FUD" for years. But more recently, two additional attitudes have crept in. These attitudes—Greed and Envy—are more corrosive to the efficient application of computer technology than anything "FUD" inspired. Greed is displayed in the understandable desire of people to possess the latest toys without consideration to cost or utility. The other is Envy that someone, someplace, might have a system with more bells and whistles. Here's how I have heard it expressed in the halls of my own company:

- *The Greed:* "I need the latest, most powerful whizzbang laptop with the greatest and latest in software and graphics. I'm pretty sure I can find a problem to solve with it."
- *The Envy:* "Jake down the hall, or our competitor down the road, has one. I should have one too."

Let me give you an example of the FUDGE factor at work at Computer Associates. I'll bet many of you have had this conversation or one like it, if not with your technology people, then probably with your children. Just recently one of my senior vice presidents stopped me in the hall. He told me that a senior VP at one of our competitors just got a 486-color laptop with 32 meg of memory, a 200-meg hard drive, Super VGA, a PCMCIA card, a fax modem, a docking station, and full-motion video with stereo speakers. In other words, one very powerful machine. "I really need one of these laptops," the VP told me.

"What do you need a machine so powerful for?" I said. "Are you planning to land the Space Shuttle?"

"But just think of how much more productive I'll be," he replied.

Of course, I know what he'll use the machine for. He'll probably use it to build presentations, maybe do a little word processing, and crunch a few spreadsheets. But mostly he'll use it for

E-mail while he's on the road. Realistically, he probably won't use more than 15–20 percent of the machine's capacity. But he had to have it. And I don't want to be unfair. He's not alone. We all do this. With everything from stereo components to cameras to computers. We all want to play with the new toy.

And that's fine. It's what hobbies were invented for. My point is that the natural human inclination for conspicuous consumption is a poor reason to invest in technology for business. If we do, we will find ourselves, at the end of the day, with technology investments that might be great fun but are not really serving any legitimate business purpose.

[Conversation]

Seven Problems with Software

Everyone needs software. It's the only thing that adds value to computer hardware and it's the only thing most of us have control over. If developed properly, it can be a meaningful competitive differentiator. It's amazing to me sometimes, given the problems with software, of just how much human ingenuity and perseverance have been able to accomplish. But it's clear to me that we won't get to a realigned environment until we solve the following seven problems with software:

1. *Maintenance—too high.* Software maintenance is like a 500-pound canary. Many organizations devote 80 percent of their programmer resources to maintaining existing software. It's a tremendous drain because software maintenance takes on a life of its own and many information technology groups can't see much past it. It's like the old joke, Do you know where a 500-pound canary sleeps? Anywhere it wants to!

2. *Reusability—too low.* We reuse machine parts and even lawyers reuse boilerplate legal language for contracts. Why is it so difficult to reuse a piece of software? The result is that software takes a long time to build and costs a fortune.

3. *Too incompatible.* Many software applications are islands of technology, unable to communicate with each other. We need the presentation of software to be designed by experts in human-machine interfaces and accepted by different developers.

4. *Too nonstandardized.* This means that hardware is expensive due to platform dependence. What we need is software that is portable across a wide spectrum of multivendor platforms.

5. *Too inconsistent.* Many software applications employ a unique look and feel that complicates training and maintenance.

6. *Too complicated.* When only programmers can create programs, everybody needs to be a programmer. The trick is to make programming of end user applications so intuitive that it makes programmers obsolete.

7. *Too focused on activities.* Most applications simply automate existing activities (paving cow paths). What's needed is software that supports business processes, such as business intelligence and teamwork.

6

How Disconnected Are You?

It's not a rhetorical question. This section explores the extent of the disconnect at your organization. The most harmful part of the disconnect is that it has remained hidden for so long.

The following pages list the most common symptoms of misalignment between business and information technology managers. As you go through the list, you will no doubt recognize symptoms that have created difficulties for your organization. Every organization exhibits the symptoms differently, but every organization exhibits some symptoms. If most of these symptoms apply to your organization, you will be especially interested in the exercise on page 50. Completing this exercise will give you a qualitative sense, perhaps for the first time, of the scope of the disconnect at your organization.

Again, lack of alignment between business and information technology in an organization is not a technology problem. It's a business problem. Manipulating the information technology department will not, by itself, eliminate the disconnect. Replacing individuals will not, by itself, eliminate the disconnect. The disconnect is a symptom of a systemic malady and nothing less than a systemic approach will bear fruit. A rational business foundation must drive realignment, and this sensible foundation must be sensibly arrived at with the participation of both business and technical management.

Gauging the Extent of the Disconnect

Before such a foundation can be mutually developed, it is useful to determine just how much damage the disconnect has done. It makes sense to gauge the extent of the disconnect between corporate management and information technology because the solution to the problem must be pegged to its scope within each organization.

[Quotation]

Having failed to distinguish thoughts from things,
we then fail to distinguish words from thoughts.
We think that if we can label a thing, we have understood it.

ANONYMOUS

Working together, representatives of corporate and technical management should come to some level of understanding about where, specifically, the disconnect has impacted the organization. They should not be afraid to answer the question: What have been the specific consequences of the disconnect? It is vital that everyone in corporate and technical management list all the misunderstandings, wasted revenue, lost opportunities, and unnecessary expenditures left in its wake. The point is not to assign blame. Blaming is just another symptom of the disconnect because it causes participants to cover themselves and snipe at each other instead of working together for the common good.

How does an organization gauge the extent of the disconnect? Fortunately or unfortunately, there are a number of well established symptoms of organizational disconnect. The exercise "How Disconnected Is Your Company?" offers an approximation of the dimensions of the disconnect at an organizational level. (CEOs may calibrate the disconnect in terms of their personal relationships with their CIOs using a similar exercise on page 71.) Here is a list of signs that information technology is not organizationally aligned with the business:

Complaints About Information Technology? Get in Line. The more pronounced the disconnect, the shriller the expressions of dissatisfaction. Some of the complaints—generally from the end users theoretically served by information technology—are over deliverables: delays in delivering applications, the lack of quality or fit of systems, excessive chargeback costs. Other complaints, generally from senior management, are generic: are we getting sufficient return from the high costs of information technology?

Senior Management: What's the Use? The silence of resignation is deafening. I much prefer outraged shouting to acquiescence of an intolerable situation. I have seen too many organizations where the disconnect is so complete that no one questions it anymore. In this situation, information technology has won the honor of bringing in-house all planning and implementation of systems. The role of the brow-beaten and resigned senior management is restricted to signing checks. The technology people think they have won, but what is it exactly that they have won? They may indeed be the masters of all they survey, but their horizons, as well as their long-term prospects, are limited.

Why Worry? I'm Here for the Paycheck. The greater the disconnect, the higher the turnover rate in the information technology organization. Information technology professionals—like every other member of an organization—want to participate in charting the enterprisewide goals of the organization. To the extent they perceive the disconnect has rendered this opportunity impossible, they feel disconnected. It is not surprising that most information technology groups display turnover rates in the range of 18 to 33 percent per year. The enterprise suffers directly and indirectly. The direct costs of turnover are expenses associated with recruitment and training. The indirect costs are less measurable but probably more profound. In companies with high turnover, people tend toward a destructively short-term attitude. What are the consequences of decisions and attitudes made by people who have a passing-through mentality?

Moreover, in information technology organizations with high turnover, the only way to conserve good people is to promote them quickly. Data centers that promote early may arguably be good for the promotee, but, from the corporate perspective, late, not early, promotion is a sign of health. Besides low turnover, late promotion means that managers are well-seasoned, can draw on a robust well of institutional memory, and can find precedent for favoring the long-term perspective.

Who's in Charge Here?   Persistent and heated conflicts between the traditional information technology function and end user departments over roles and responsibilities indicate the operation of a fundamental disconnect. One common pattern in these cases is that a growing number of end user departments elect to liberate themselves from the information technology function, preferring to fill their information needs internally or through contracting with services outside the organization. Another widespread symptom of ongoing internal conflict is the persistent attractiveness that outsourcing part or all of the information technology function has among the organization's senior managers.

You Go Your Way, I'll Go Mine.   Where is the enterprisewide vision? In this case, the disconnect has led to dispersal of information technology to the business units (which may possibly be good) but without the requisite, high-level coordination (which is indubitably bad). While the business units in isolation may exhibit a high degree of information technology effectiveness and may prosper from their self-reliance, an appropriate cross-functional vision and information technology architecture does not exist. An inevitable result of isolation is islands of automation, where the systems and applications of one group can neither share common data nor exchange information with other groups. Without coordination at the enterprise level, the outcome is the balkanization of information technology resources, resulting in the inability of the organization to respond to enterprise-level opportunities.

Department of Redundancy Department. Duplication of effort is another dimension of a lack of enterprisewide vision. When multiple groups in an organization embark on information technology projects, it is inevitable that they will independently replicate applications. The results are unfortunate for two main reasons. First, as already noted, the systems will almost certainly be incompatible, developed on different hardware platforms using different architectures. The unnecessary cost of redundancy can be considerable, the scant reuse of information wasteful. But more significant are the opportunity costs of the precious time squandered by all that parallel development, time that a more aligned competitor no doubt has used to advantage.

How Can They Do That? We Couldn't! One consequence of the disconnect is that the organization is unable to focus the appropriate business and information technology resources in a relevant time frame. And its aligned competitors can. When business unit managers see their competitors leapfrog them through the innovative use of information technology, the disconnect is usually a considerable factor in the equation.

Organizations that align information technology with corporate goals consistently deliver more competitive products and services. They are quick to market, have lower costs, and make the right decisions most of the time. Relative to disconnected companies, aligned organizations also:

- Spend less on consultants.
- Outsource less often.
- Are faster to market.
- React more responsively to changing conditions.

Well Positioned on the Bleeding Edge.   If you prepare a skill set inventory of the technical professionals in the information technology resource (not a bad idea in any event), what would you find? You would find a staff desperate to exploit the latest technologies and architectures, presumably distributed computing, local area networks, client/server solutions, and object-oriented programming techniques, rather than focusing on the needs of the business. The organization would occupy a well publicized position on the bleeding edge of technology and the information technology people would be celebrated as pioneers. The requirements of the business would take the back seat to a pattern of technology for technology's sake.

[Exercise]

How Disconnected Is Your Company?

Every business foundation has a unique balance between corporate and technical management. Your responses to the following 10 questions will indicate the role of information technology in your organization.

1. Over half of the application projects started in the last 12 months were never delivered.
   [ ] Agree   [ ] Disagree   [ ] No Opinion
2. Over half of the application projects delivered in the last 12 months were late.
   [ ] Agree   [ ] Disagree   [ ] No Opinion

3. Over half of the application projects delivered in the last six months were over budget.
   [ ] Agree   [ ] Disagree   [ ] No Opinion

4. Turnover in the information technology organization exceeds 15 percent per year.
   [ ] Agree   [ ] Disagree   [ ] No Opinion

5. Strategic information technology planning is conducted *without* substantial input from senior corporate management.
   [ ] Agree   [ ] Disagree   [ ] No Opinion

6. More than 10 percent of business units buy information technology services from noncorporate entities.
   [ ] Agree   [ ] Disagree   [ ] No Opinion

7. Business units work without an enterprisewide information technology architecture and standards.
   [ ] Agree   [ ] Disagree   [ ] No Opinion

8. Two or more business units have independently developed applications that are substantially similar in function or scope.
   [ ] Agree   [ ] Disagree   [ ] No Opinion

9. The senior information technology executive and the CEO have not had a substantive face-to-face meeting in the last six months.
   [ ] Agree   [ ] Disagree   [ ] No Opinion

10. A competitor's advantage can be traced to the innovative use of information technology.
   [ ] Agree   [ ] Disagree   [ ] No Opinion

Scoring: Score one point for every question you agreed with.

0–2 The synergy between information technology and enterprise strategy is world-class. There is little in this (or in any other book on information technology) that can assist you.

3–4 You represent a leading-edge organization in the alignment of information and corporate strategy. You need fear little from your competitors.

5–7   Your information technology resource is squarely in the tradi-
      tion of American data centers in the mid-1990s. A number
      of troubling issues need to be addressed if your organiza-
      tion is not to be left behind.

8–10 There is a massive disconnect at work between the informa-
      tion technology and corporate managers. It is likely that prof-
      its, quality, and market share are all at risk. Immediate atten-
      tion to the disconnect issue is paramount.

7

It's a Great Idea.
I Don't Like It.

One of the most perverse aspects of human nature is that no matter how desirable an outcome, no matter how deplorable the status quo, significant numbers of people always resist change. CEOs who attempt to eliminate the disconnect will find a number of forces arrayed in its defense. The CEO should be sensitive to this point:

*Changing the information technology system
in the slightest way alters the distribution of power.*

Resistance to change is so predictable that some far-sighted organizations actually offer seminars that teach employees how to overcome resistance. The idea is that if resistance is so predictable, let's acknowledge it, look at it boldly, and learn from it. "It can be extremely useful and constructive to bring to the surface the fact that resistance is a natural process," says Vaughn Merlyn at Ernst & Young's Center for Information Strategy and Technology in Boston.

The reasons that people are resisting are often valid. The resistance is always there; it has to be addressed. Employees can really contribute to the overall success of the change program by talking about the things that concern them. Often the things that concern them are valid concerns.

The job of the CEO is to build coalitions. CEOs in other parts of the world do this much better than the average American CEO. The Japanese CEO, for example, recognizes that the corporation is a political institution. We shy away from that perspective in America. We call it "playing politics" and think of it as somehow tainted. American executives would do well to consider politics the art of influencing their colleagues in the organization. "When an organization faces complex decisions, politics becomes instrumental because of the relationship between the positions and agendas of different people," says Peter Burris, Director of Worldwide Commercial Systems Research for International Data Corporation in Framingham, Mass.

> Organizations are in place to minimize the impacts and the risks associated with the failure of any single decision. Politics are in place to ensure that information is made available to the decision-making process and that a consensus can be built where it should be built in a way that reflects the overall stakes of the decision to be made.

The CIO also has a political role to play. Managing the communications highways that enable the connected organization becomes a deeply political responsibility. Computer technology has flattened the organization, eliminating layers and bringing executives and workers closer together. Computer technology has facilitated communications across functional and hierarchical boundaries previously closed to easy communication. It has made it easier to bring together physically remote individuals that have similar expertise. It has also made it easier to mold individuals with dissimilar expertise into effective decision-making teams. All these factors promote organizations that can align information technology with strategic corporate goals.

[Interview]

Resisting the Disconnect

Charles, organizational resistance is a fact of life. Sometimes the harder the CEO pushes, the harder the system pushes back. What can a CEO do in the face of resistance?

The CEO can make a change at the CIO level. The purpose of information technology is to serve the business. If the CEO pushes to get more alignment with information technology and the CIO resists, you are at cross purposes. You have to make a change.

What is the CIO really saying when he or she resists?

The same old song: "We're different; you don't understand us; you can't talk to us; we're elite; you're idiots." I was a programmer, so I know this firsthand. We actually thought we were a different breed.

Will replacing the CIO fix the problem?

It depends on whom you bring in. If you bring in the right leader—a businessperson first, a technologist second—sure.

Did you ever see such resistance at CA?

Sure, let me set up the situation. My theory about controlling costs at CA is very simple: Employees spend money. So if I watch how many people I have, I'll contain costs. I decided that I would personally keep and update the organization charts of the company. Until a few years ago, I maintained all the organization charts on a PC. It took me about four hours a month. Some people call that crazy, but I learned some important things.

What did you learn?

If you keep the employee count at the number you're supposed to, you're fine. I also discovered which of my managers managed by the organization chart. Anyway, back to your question. There was a talented technical guy who was building a new product support team and we got into this big battle. He insisted he needed 13 people. To me, he needed eight. So I gave him his organization chart with eight empty boxes. Well, he wasn't happy. He went to human resources, he went to R&D, he went everywhere trying to get some help for his position that he needed not eight but 13 positions. He drove everybody nuts.

How did you handle it?

Finally, I called him in and gave him a new organization chart. It had 13 empty boxes. I said, "You won, okay? I'll give you 13 people. But do me a favor, when you hire the eighth person, will you just come and see me?" Well, he never came back. He hired six people and did a beautiful job.

The moral of the story?

I see two morals. First, it takes two people to sustain a battle. There's always a way to diffuse any conflict without giving in.

And the second moral?

The disconnect occurs when you are working the system instead of attending to the customer. I say your job is not to fill out the organization chart. Your job is to provide the customer service. Keep your eyes on the customer and start doing the job even if you don't have all the resources you think you need.

Is this a problem with technical people?

Not exclusively. I've seen many wonderfully trained managers fresh out of business school who can't get started until the organization chart is completely filled up.

[Quotation]

There is no way to make people like change.
You can only make them feel less threatened by it.

FREDERICK O.R. HAYES
Nineteenth-century New York City politician

8

Aligning Business Strategy and Information Technology Strategy

Over the past three years, numerous surveys and studies of executive managers have been consistent in one dimension: The number one issue for both CEOs and CIOs is how to align the company's information technology strategy with its business strategy. As recently as 1989, according to the Index Group, this issue didn't even make the top five issues of concern to CEOs. But today, executives on both sides of the aisle rightfully have an almost physical sense that this strategic alignment supersedes practically everything else if they are to utilize information technology to maximum effectiveness.

Information technology professionals have frequently been criticized for being massively indifferent to the market forces that drive the businesses that employ them. This accusation was especially true back in the 1960s and 1970s, when centralized mainframes, with their attendant elite group of programmers and systems analysts who were all too often more interested in the computer than in the organization, dominated many firms. In today's competitive environment, no organization can afford such an indulgence.

To their credit, information technology professionals now appear to have recognized this unforgiving fact, and have become more focused on their businesses. The emphasis on modern information technology practices such as downsizing (see page 145), client/server computing (page 149), and business process reengineering (page 176) indicate that many firms are actively connecting information systems more closely with the business.

It is beyond the scope of this book to map how organizations can mesh information technology initiatives and strategic operational plans. Nevertheless, it is useful for CEOs and CIOs alike to consider the merits of redefining the way information technology plans are formulated.

If your business is typical, the business plan comes first, followed by the information technology plan. But there are definite advantages to developing the business plans and information technology plans concurrently. A number of information-intensive industries, acknowledging the centrality of their information resources to their businesses, have found that by developing these plans simultaneously, they can achieve much tighter integration of information technology into the core requirements of the organization.

Consider also the advantages of actually leading the planning process with information technology requirements. A few organizations use the information technology planning process to identify opportunities that drive the development of the business. A classic example is AMR Corp., the parent company of American Airlines, which now plans opportunities around the centrality of its SABRE reservation system. A more recent example of strategic alignment of information technology with business is MCI's Friends and Family program. This remarkably successful program is a seamless marriage between MCI's information and telecommunications networks and its marketing strategy to pioneer innovative services—in this case developing market share by providing discounts to subscribers when they call friends and family members. One indicator of the success of MCI's strategy, as well as its implementation, is that all of its competitors have followed suit with similar programs.

[Speech to CIOs]

Get Your Noses Out of the Data Center

Never have you been better prepared to lead your organizations through the challenges of the last decade of the twentieth century.

The information technology managers who will succeed are those that get their noses out of the data center and can articulate an understanding of long-term company business requirements. This new role requires a different skill set and a different mind set. The manager has to be able to look beyond data and move past the technical issues of generating information, although these processes obviously remain important. If managers are to be accepted as partners in corporate management, they must demonstrate their problem-solving abilities to colleagues in Operations, Finance, and every other area.

For information technology managers, that means making full use of their interpersonal and communications skills, as well as their analytical skills. It also means being involved, being assertive, and reaching out to help the organization become more profitable and more competitive.

Shifting the attitude of an information technologist from that of a technical authority to that of a knowledgeable consultant requires considerable retraining. Offering alternatives requires more effort than imposing restrictions, and this effort should be rewarded. Compensation policies that reward rigid, autocratic attitudes should be realigned to offer incentives for the cross-functional, process-oriented attitudes that encourage creativity and flexibility.

Part 2
Realignment

Many senior executives have fundamentally lost faith in the ability of information technology to offer a durable competitive edge. It's not because today's technology isn't powerful enough. We have more technology than we can handle. There is so much power and functionality in the technology available today, that most of it is not used to capacity. It's not because of the incompetence of the people hired for the care and feeding of computers. In fact, they have done a superb job in building ultrareliable machines and systems. The loss of faith is a result of the disconnect between the objectives and priorities of the people running businesses and the technologists.

The Information Age imposes new realities on business organizations. The old ways of doing business, which assumed a constant, predictable environment, simply don't work anymore. In addition, the processes involved in producing or delivering goods and services have become increasingly complicated. Managing these processes, especially in a constantly changing and unpredictable environment, tests even the best decision-making teams.

In today's brutal economic environment, any division between an enterprise's executive and technical staffs is too costly. Strategic planning to meet the demands of the global, time-compressed economy is impossible without pioneering information technology initiatives tightly aligned with busi-

ness goals. Success requires maximum cooperation and understanding between CEOs and CIOs. Fortunately, as I have personally witnessed, an increasing number of CEOs and CIOs
are taking positive steps to bridge the gap between their staffs.

The best way to bridge the gap is for the representatives of
executive and information technology management to start
with zero-based thinking. Look at the partnership and its activities. For each activity, ask the following questions:

- Does this activity have value?
- How does it affect our clients and what they are asking us to
  do for them?
- Why are we doing it?
- If we stop doing it, what will happen?
- Should we be doing something else instead?

In other words, the partnership between CEOs and CIOs
must be completely renegotiated. If the relationship between
CEOs and CIOs is to be transformed, both sides will have to
reexamine every assumption, every behavior, and every practice defended by tradition and common sense in the light of
whether these practices support the desired outcome. Some
people call the process I have just described business process
reengineering. At Computer Associates, we call it *reinvention*.

I will discuss business process reengineering in Chap. 21.
For now let me say only that, when you continually reinvent
your processes, people, and technology, there is little or no
need for the expense and upheaval that business process reengineering inevitably exacts. At Computer Associates, we ask
these questions—not annually or every several years—but
continually. The answers might mean that we have to change
what we're doing or how we're doing it, but we're not afraid
to make those changes and do it quickly.

Part 1 of the book examined the development of the disconnect and its consequences. This, the second part, concerns itself with realignment of the organization. It outlines the spe-

cific areas of the partnership between CEOs and CIOs that will have to be restructured if there is to be a dent made in the disconnect. I take a zero-based approach. Starting from scratch means no sacred cows. This section puts every element of the CEO-CIO partnership on the table.

I consider it obvious that the CEO has ultimate responsibility for eliminating the disconnect between the corporate and technical management of the company. It can be no other way because the chief executive, by definition, has ultimate responsibility for everything connected with the enterprise. That said, the responsibility for combating the disconnect must be personally accepted by everyone in corporate and technical management.

[Quotation]

A CEO in a ten-foot hole is not well served by a CIO who offers a six-foot rope and then can't understand why the CEO is still frustrated. After all, he's met the CEO more than half-way.

CHARLES B. WANG
Chairman and CEO, Computer Associates International

9
Foundations for Realignment

We are witness to an immense shake-up transforming corporate America. Organizations in the 1990s are refocusing their efforts around access to information. Until a few years ago, most centralized organizations relied on research and development and marketing to stimulate growth. Today, with the increasing emphasis on decentralized business units and the rate of technological change in our global economy, technology and information have become as critical as R&D and marketing as keys to future success. Companies that thrive and survive in our global marketplace will be information-based. Millions of dollars, including the survival of the company, are on the line to a much more intense degree than ever before. Without accurate data, companies are more at risk for every decision that must be made.

For at least the last 10 years senior business and information systems executives have struggled with how to bring information technology and business into closer alignment. As business needs multiplied and the gap widened between the solutions information technology offered and the business challenges managers faced, enlightened representatives of both camps redoubled their commitment to ending the disconnect. The ideal they have been striving toward is an alignment that will optimize the provision of information technology and service to the user community.

The focus of information systems has changed from automating internal (back room) processes to enabling multifaceted mechanisms for directly delivering products or services to the customer. The increased complexity of these systems is compounded by the fact that many are used for competitive advantage, giving them life-or-death urgency. The central argument now becomes how to organize information technology to achieve higher levels of competitive advantage.

With today's shorter product cycles, the old information technology culture leads inevitably to large development backlogs and missed delivery targets. Corporate efforts to hold down total information technology costs also are symptomatic of the old mentality and can be problematic, given strenuous business unit competition for available, sometimes even scarce, information technology resources.

Notwithstanding a greater melding of information technology and business units, alignment efforts must maintain standards for professional information technology work and systems, and allow information technology professionals practical career options. If you can get opportunity and technology together, you have a better chance to identify competitive-advantage systems.

Companies that have internalized these new realities have substantially eliminated the disconnect. Sometimes they are termed *learning organizations*. Others call them *virtual organizations*. By whatever name they are called, these companies have the ability to access and process information on global competitive intelligence, new product information, research and development, market trends, and environmental and regulatory impacts. Having done so, they can quickly act and then move on to the next challenge. Eliminating the disconnect removes many of the obstacles that keep today's organizations paralyzed.

[Quotation]

If you have built castles in the air, your work need not be lost; that is where they should be. Now put foundations under them.

HENRY DAVID THOREAU
American naturalist and writer, 1817–1862

Many methods for aligning information technology resources and business goals are already in use at many companies. I am privileged to visit hundreds of companies every year and I have observed many methods and strategies for aligning business and technology. My conclusion is that there are as many strategies as there are companies. Every organization presents a unique set of constraints and opportunities. Yet in the course of visits to companies large and small, I have found that a core set of business strategies is common to the most successful companies. I have identified five key strategies that learning organizations can take to eliminate the disconnect. A combination of these methods is probably the best guarantee of across-the-board success because each of these strategies has its own inherent risks. The five steps are:

1. Select the right CIO.
2. Decentralize and disperse information technology resources.
3. Transform information technology to a profit center.
4. Advance end user computing.
5. Promote evolution, not revolution.

1. Select the Right CIO

I am convinced that, while most CEOs are keen judges of character, most don't have a clue about how to recruit a CIO. Two things need to be kept in mind.

First, selecting the chief information technology executive is a job a CEO cannot delegate. If you're going to have a CIO as one of your top echelon managers, and if you're committed to having a close working partnership, then you have to select the CIO yourself.

Second, you have to ask one fundamental question about each CIO candidate: Is this person CEO material? It seems to me that, if this key question can be answered affirmatively, there is a good chance for the beginnings of a true partnership between the CEO and the CIO.

[Quotation]

The term CIO doesn't mean anything. I'm not the chief of information. At best, I am the chief of processes that provide and distribute information. I don't create information, I rarely manage it, and I certainly don't own it.

DEAN O. ALLEN
Vice President of Information and Administrative Services,
Lockheed Corporation, Calabasas, California

Nevertheless, too many CEOs still perceive information technology as automating manual processes. Until they see it as a weapon to be more competitive, they will be tempted to ask their CFOs to pick the CIO. This is the practice in a little less than half the companies that attended "The CEO In a Wired World" Conferences discussed in Chap. 12. Most companies have information technology reporting to the financial executive. The disconnect cannot be eliminated until this practice is retired and CEOs take personal responsibility to select the organization's CIO.

[Conversation]

*If the Top Rung on the CIO Career
Ladder Doesn't Lead to at Least Your Job, Why Not?*

At a recent conference attended by some 120 CIOs, I asked a simple question: How many of you would be considered for a CEO job or are in the upper echelons of executive management where you deal with the CEO?

I think three hands went up.

It was scary. The question becomes, where do you guys go? You're not going to be CEO or join the upper echelons of executive management. What is left unsaid is that you have a professional career; you don't have a business career. And that should scare the hell out of you.

Here's my advice to CEOs: If you don't take those technology people and move them into your upper echelons to become part of your strategic planning, you're not using technology. I don't care what you say—you're not using it, and you're not going to use it.

The bottom line is that eliminating the disconnect requires a change of attitude. Both the CEO and CIO have to accept a new outlook. The CEO's responsibility is to learn some technology and open up the decision-making process. The CIO's contract is to accept the role of the businessperson chiefly responsible for making the technology serve the business. If the CEO accepts the role of leading this change and the CIO accepts that his or her role is to deliver solutions and relevant information, all properly wrapped to meet the needs of the business, the disconnect will dissolve and be replaced by a new partnership.

[Joke]

Two CEOs are talking after a game of tennis. The first one says, "How come Mike [the CIO] is not your double's partner anymore?"

"Would you be a partner with a guy who doesn't know information technology from a hole in the ground, second guesses your every move, and blames you for every setback?" says the other CEO.

"Of course not."

"Well, neither would Mike."

[Interview]

Interviewing a CIO

Charles, you need to hire a new CIO. The candidates are waiting outside, and you can ask each of them just three questions.

What's the first question?

Would you like to run my company?

What's the right answer?

The right answer is, "It depends."

What's the last answer you want to hear?

"No, no no. I'm really interested in running a highly distributed UNIX environment." What you have here is a technical professional, perhaps a good one, but not CIO material.

What is the second question?

What happened to the business at the company you last served?

What's the worst case answer to this one?

"It was great. We put in a distributed, relational, client-server OS/2 application over an Ethernet LAN using TCP/IP." I immediately translate this gobbledygook to mean, "Well, we're closing the business and that's why I'm looking for a new job." But wait. Actually, there's even a worse answer to this question. Just thinking about it makes me ill.

We'll risk it.

"I outsourced myself out of a job." It's the biggest crock in the world.

How about question number three?

Have you ever worked for a company where you came in and said, "That's pretty good. Leave it alone. Don't mess with it."?

What's the worst case answer?

"No, my job is to always improve on the existing system. If it ain't broke, fix it, that's what I say." Don't walk, run away from this cowboy. These people are sure there's always room for improvement and are willing to bet all the money I have to prove it.

Earlier in this book, CEOs had a chance to calculate the disconnect at the organizational level ("How Disconnected is Your Company?"). The following exercise allows CEOs to judge the extent of the disconnect on the primary relationship between CEOs and CIOs.

[Exercise]

A Disconnect Checklist for CEOs

1. Do you trust your CIO's judgment? (If your answer is no, skip this exercise. You have a different problem altogether.)

2. Does your CIO report directly to you?

3. Does your CIO proactively meet the business challenges of your organization?

4. Has your CIO drawn up a clear technology plan for the 1990s? (Give yourself one bonus point if you have actually read this plan; give yourself another bonus point if you actually understood it.)

5. Has your CIO tried to brief you and the board of directors on this plan? (Give yourself one bonus point if you actually held the meeting.)

6. Has a complete cost/benefit analysis of the plan been done?

7. Does the technology plan leverage off the existing information system resources?

8. Does your CIO consider outsourcing companies a benchmark against which to measure the company's own performance?

9. Has your CIO built a robust network infrastructure that can reliably handle the workload of distributed computing?

10. Has your CIO made a defensible case for downsizing to smaller platforms to reduce dependence on the mainframe? (If not, give yourself one bonus point if the CIO has made a defensible case for retaining the mainframe.)

Scoring: Score one point for each yes.

11–14	You're very lucky, but why aren't you taking your CIO out to lunch? He's probably being actively recruited by the competition.
7–10	Your CIO is squarely in the tradition of most contemporary CIOs.
4–6	Your CIO is struggling. Consider looking for a new CIO.
0–4	Consider a new CEO.

[Quotation]

It's futile for sheep to pass resolutions in favor of vegetarianism when wolves are of a different opinion.   ANONYMOUS

---

2. Decentralize and Disperse Information Technology Resources

Many companies have looked to decentralize or disperse information technology resources to better align business and technical objectives. In solving some problems, decentralization and dispersal introduce others just as troublesome.

Decentralization is a broadly used term. I use it to refer to the process whereby a large central information technology group is broken up, physically placed with the business groups they support, but still report to a central information technology unit. Thus while they are physically decentralized, there is no decentralization of management authority. While these groups are still managed by information technology professionals, the information technology resource is brought closer to the business units and their customers. This can only be good for the company, although the administrative challenges are intensified.

Dispersed information technology decentralizes management responsibility as well as physically relocating the people. The information technology professionals generally report to the managers in the business departments and workgroups they serve. The result can be a very tight integration of technology and business applications. Often there is a dotted line relationship between the dispersed information technology groups and a central group responsible for information technology standards.

There are a number of problems with decentralization. In many cases, decentralization does not address the alignment problem because systems are still developed according to traditional methodologies. The disconnect is still in high gear. Instead of one big disconnect, the company has created a number of smaller disconnects. Another downside is enforcing discipline and standards among the autonomous business units. For all its limitations, the centralized data processing function did develop an impressive record for maintaining data integrity, data security, the enforcement of standards, and backup in case of disaster. There is ample evidence that decentralized processing has trouble with these fundamental elements of systems management.

My experience is that decentralized information technology units establish their own standards and procedures, often without regard to the rest of the enterprise. Without a strong CIO, communication among the decentralized units breaks down. Turnover in information technology can also become more of a problem in decentralized units. While an information technology professional's career need not be interrupted by decentralization, information technology groups relocated to business units can sometimes be ostracized and relegated to out-of-the-way corners, bypassed by increasingly sophisticated end users. Consequently, this kind of reorganization, without explicit attention to the culture, actually worsens the alignment situation.

Providing practical career options for decentralized information technology professionals may be the most difficult issue. In some decentralized organizations, many information technology professionals feel lost in the business units. Many technical professionals feel constrained because decentralization limits or terminates as many technical careers as it forges. Technical professionals know this. As a result, turnover can be high in the first few months following decentralization. On the other hand, some technical professionals enthusiastically learn the business and make a home for themselves on the business side. This outcome has value for both the individual and the organization. For the individual, a business mentality can only have survival value in today's economy. For the organization, the combination of up-to-date technical skills with a sound business outlook makes for a valued contributor.

[Conversation]

The Center Sometimes Holds

People think that just because you decentralize, you get more productive and save money.

Wrong.

Too often, companies decentralize to hide responsibility and costs. I remember a CIO of a Fortune 1000 company boasting, "You know, we decentralized and I took my staff from 25 people to 2." Now, I happen to know about this company. The central information technology staff did go from 25 people to 2. But what the CIO forgot to mention was that the company quickly added 40 people in the various user departments to handle the same amount of work.

Dispersing information technology to user departments has considerable benefits, but don't expect to reduce staff in the process.

3. Transform Information Technology to a Profit Center

Another method for alignment is to convert the information technology resource into a profit center. The idea is to make explicit the service nature of the information technology resource. In theory, the information technology department has to demonstrate its value to the other business units. In practice, the data center usually retains enough captive business to maintain itself, thus defeating the value of making information technology dependent on free market economics. To help focus the information technology resource, users should have the option of contracting with the service that offers the best terms. When competition drives prices down and quality up, everyone benefits.

This strategy can, unfortunately, create a new set of contractual walls between information technology and the user. But if the contracting process is managed well, user departments are much better off than when they were the captive customers of an often indifferent information technology center.

An extension to this approach is to spin off information technology as a separate business entity altogether. This sink-or-swim approach can transform inefficient data centers into models of productivity and can even return a profit to the parent company. The downside is that it forces the data center to focus much more energy on marketing as it pursues business opportunities.

I haven't seen making information technology an independent profit center done well. In his introduction to this book, Peter Drucker regrets coining the term "profit center." His well-taken point is that, in the context of the business isolated from the customer, the very concept of the profit center is suspicious. "Profit comes only .from the outside," he writes. "When the customer returns with a repeat order and his check doesn't bounce, then you have a profit center. Until then you have only cost centers." Spinning off information technology accomplishes little unless rigorous commitments to marketing, customer service, quality, and other business objectives accompany the spin-off.

4. Advance End-User Computing

An emphasis on end user computing helps align business goals with information technology because it puts both decisions into the hands of the people with the most intimate understanding of the business challenges. End user computing offloads information processing work to the users with the business expertise and lets them decide how best to do it. The benefits are immediate: Users get the system they want because they themselves have built it. Since they are totally invested in the process, the resulting systems have a greater chance of being on target and more likely to stay on time and on budget.

The principal problem with end user computing is that end user groups have not developed the data center disciplines that have been found to make for reliable, secure, and robust applications. Systems developed by end users frequently suffer from data security and integrity issues. Maintenance of professional standards for data backups, for example, are frequently neglected, which can be a fatal flaw for business-critical systems.

The good news is that emerging system software will help end users prepare applications that are as reliable and maintainable as those developed by professional programmers. The key is to determine what kinds of systems end users can be expected to develop reasonably well and how best to help them develop them. The goal is not to turn end users into programmers. There is no percentage in that. Rather, the goal is to give end users tools they can use to access the information they need more easily. This access can be achieved by making people with pertinent programming skills available to end users as mentors. A side benefit to that is that end users learn more about information technology, and the programming staff learns more about business goals. A favored strategy (see the previous section) is to place information technology in the business unit, either temporarily or permanently, but having it still report to central information technology.

Success depends on being able to move the information technology professional into a consulting role to deal with cleanup and documentation requirements for business-critical systems. In any case, it does not seem likely or desirable that end user computing can manage large, real-time host-based operational systems. So it addresses only part of the business unit performance issue.

[Anecdote]

Do We Really Need Another Paper Cutter?

In the late 1980s, when the subject of the proliferation of PCs was a major concern, a leading analyst in the PC world had a memorable exchange with a Vice President of Information Systems at a Fortune 500 corporation. "How many PCs are there in this company?" she asked the executive.

The VP of IS was quick to answer: 267.

This number seemed low to her so she asked, "How do you know?"

"Because I have to approve every PC purchase," he said. They then went on to other matters.

Her question must have touched off something, because a couple of days later he phoned the analyst. "I was wrong," he said. "We have over 1100 PCs and we're still counting."

How could he have been so wrong? In order to avoid having to go through IS, end users purchased PCs but called them calculators, desk accessories, typewriters, imaging equipment, even paper cutters, almost anything but PCs.

The lesson she took from this experience was simple: Information technology professionals cannot stand in the way of end us-

ers. End users will have their way, if for no other reason than because they have the money.

I am indebted to AMY WOHL,
Bala Cynwid, Pennsylvania, for this anecdote.

---

5. Promote Evolution,
Not Revolution

One consequence of the disconnect is an unthinking preference
for revolution. I hope you will resist it. I believe in a different
approach. I believe it is almost criminal to destroy existing
technology simply because something new comes along. Something new will always be coming along. But it will rarely be in
the best interests of your business to abandon what is working
well and risk replacing it with something that might work better.
The approach I favor is called *intelligent evolution*.

Think evolution, not revolution. Rethink how you can use
existing technology, and you may find that you don't need to
discard the old after all. Evolution limits risk while enabling the
introduction of new technologies integrated with existing systems so that your company can continue to be responsive to the
competitive demands of the market.

A case in point: Due to a rapidly expanding client base,
National Bancard Corporation (Nabanco) had to find an alternative to its manual method of handling customer calls and
recording service inquiries. Certain elements within the company were tempted by a radical new systems approach to the
challenge. Instead, cooler heads prevailed. Nabanco realized it
had powerful tools for managing the data center where customer service calls were professionally serviced and recorded;
what it needed was a way to extend those tools to the environment outside the data center. That is exactly what Nabanco did.
It leveraged its existing investments and expertise. By applying
new thinking to existing technology, Nabanco gave a big push
to its customer service capabilities. Moreover, with an evolution-

ary approach, it did so considerably cheaper and faster than anything a revolutionary alternative promised.

[Speech]

Intelligent Evolution

History and science tell us that there are two basic courses: revolution or evolution. The revolutionaries would suggest that the only way to take advantage of new technology is to throw away everything we've done so far and start from scratch.

But imagine leveling a building every time you wanted to add a new door or central air conditioning. It's the same thing with implementing new technology. Destroying the old to add something new just doesn't make sense. Listening to the revolutionaries may be inspiring, but you have to temper their advice with common sense.

I believe that there's an approach that will work. I call it intelligent evolution. And the approach involves the simple concept of building. It involves taking the technology that we know works as a foundation, and building on that foundation by adding the new technology. Is that not the way the world has always adapted to new environments? Through evolution?

The most important aspect of this approach is that it respects and lets you leverage the significant investments you've already made in information technology. There is tremendous value in building on the investments in technology and know-how that have already been made. And it's the builders, not the revolutionaries, that make our businesses grow. We've always taken this approach at CA and have built a very successful business around this strategy.

Once you've begun to think in terms of protecting current investments in information technology and how to extend the technology already in place, you'll find many innovative solutions that would never pass muster with the revolutionaries, but that can add value to your business. I also submit that solutions based on protecting current investments are far more appealing from a financial perspective, especially in today's sensitive economic climate, and are less disruptive to day-to-day operations.

10

Ten Steps for Improved CEO/CIO Relationships

Having agreed to eliminate the disconnect between corporate and technical management, what can CEOs do to bridge the gulf and really make technology work for the company? The following is by no means a definitive list, but it represents a foundation for establishing and maintaining productive working relationships between business and information technology managers. The ten steps are:

1. Keep all eyes on the prize.
2. Realign information technology as a team player.
3. Transform information technology methodologies.
4. Increase CIO participation in strategic planning sessions.
5. Overcome the techno-illiteracy crisis.

6. Foster an environment in which mistakes are welcome.

7. The facts are friendly: insist on the truth.

8. Without trust, everything is friction.

9. Rank the information technology managers.

10. Have fun.

1. Keep All Eyes on the Prize

Many CEOs have been frustrated by the inability of the CIOs to articulate strategic technical issues in the quantifiable and financial business terms that CEOs rely on. Worse still, some CEOs have been repeatedly frustrated by the missed deadlines, blown budgets, and lost business opportunities that have characterized their companies' information technology initiatives.

On the upper right-hand corner of every white board of every analyst and project manager in the information technology department, the following two statements should be written:

1. Information technology has no other legitimate role than to support the business of the enterprise.

2. The answer to the question (in 25 words or less), What is the business objective of my company?

This exercise will help everyone remember to challenge any assumption that information technology is important on its own merits, apart from its contribution to the enterprise's business objectives. It will also encourage everyone to pledge eternal vigilance against information technology initiatives that are not strictly aligned with the clearly stated company objective.

These two statements don't exactly represent radical ideas, but many information technology people find them hard to swallow. Many technical people still believe that their primary goal is the care and feeding of the corporate information systems. This impression must be corrected, and there is no one to do it but the CEO. The technologists may resist at first, but they will thank you for it later.

[Conversation]

You Can't Tell Who's Winning
by Watching the Scoreboard

Good financial results do not necessarily represent good performance. Rather, they are the consequence of good performance.

What measure of corporate performance, then, should information technology managers scrutinize? Consider a baseball analogy. How do you know whether your team is winning? The scoreboard may tell you who was ahead an instant ago. But if you keep your eyes on the scoreboard, you'll watch the score change—and it won't be in your favor. You play good baseball by keeping your eyes on your teammates, the opposing players, and, most of all, the ball. There is enough time to look at the scoreboard between innings.

Obviously, the scoreboard of the enterprise—the profit and loss statements, cash flow figures, and other traditional financial measures—are still relevant. But many corporations now recognize the need to track nonfinancial measurements of performance too, and they are asking information technology managers to work with other areas of the organization to provide that information. To stay competitive, they want to track variables like on-time shipments, employee turnover, defects, manufacturing cycle time, and product development cycle time. The information technology manager who can deliver these items or—better yet—anticipate their need will become valued partners in the management of the enterprise.

[Quotation]

Be wiser than other people if you can, but do not tell them so.
LORD CHESTERFIELD
British statesman, 1694-1773

2. Realign Information Technology as a Team Player

Old paradigms die hard. The old paradigm of information technology as an inflexible, reactive processor of customer requests must yield to a new attitude of involvement and teamwork. No longer should information technology staff develop systems and solutions based on system requirements framed by analysts who are not directly working with the application. Instead, information technology staff should be involved in customer applications as early as possible, visiting customer sites to learn the requirements firsthand and to educate end users about their choices in meeting them.

[Joke]

The Salesman and the Pig

A computer salesman is traveling along a country road when he sees a farmer staggering under the weight of an enormous pig. Amazed, the salesman stops his car and sees that the farmer is holding the pig above his head so that the fat animal can eat the acorns off an oak tree.

"Excuse me," he says to the farmer, "but if you'd put that pig down and shake the tree, the acorns would fall to the ground. It would really save quite a lot of time."

"Maybe," the farmer says, "But what's time to a pig?"

A simple but effective way to do this is to shift ownership of information technology projects and eliminate incentives that encourage empire building and delays in delivering applications. The following principles address this shift:

- Information technology projects should be owned by the customer groups whose requirements they address.

- Incentives for the information technology group must be linked to delivering applications as quickly as possible.

When end users accept ownership of a project, the politics of developing systems magically improves. "Their" system suddenly becomes "our" system. Delays or sloppiness that users justified when the system was someone else's responsibility are no longer tolerated when inconveniencing your own workgroup. When users have a vested interest in completing the project, their approval process takes less time and delivery schedules can be streamlined. If users realize that they will be the ones who live with any bugs or limitations, they make more time available to define requirements and review project progress. Finally, as users participate more in their "owned" projects, they better understand their own requirements, as well as the issues and constraints facing their information technology partners. Subsequent projects flow more smoothly, reflecting the users' growing participation in every area of the system development life cycle.

3. Transform Information Technology Methodologies

If information technology hopes to develop relevant and successful applications, it has to respond much faster to emerging business needs than ever before. The more volatile business requirements become, the more flexible and responsive information technology needs to be.

Traditional methodologies simply will not meet rapidly changing business requirements. CIOs that grew up in technocentric data centers must learn the new paradigms for addressing business problems. CIOs that rose to their current positions from noninformation technology disciplines must familiarize themselves with both old and new complex technologies. In either case, they have a learning curve to climb in order to become conversant with new tools and techniques, to see if they have merit in helping meet business objectives.

The ability to deliver results quickly has enormous implications. Once information technology has attained this credibility, CEOs will realize that if they have a dream, information technology can build it. Otherwise, when it takes two years to design and implement anything, a CEO's dream is merely a fantasy.

4. Increase CIO Participation in Strategic Planning Sessions

At this point in business evolution, every organization has, no doubt, resolved the question of whether or not to have an individual take the title of Chief Information Officer (CIO). Some companies prefer Chief Technology Officer. Other titles are VP, Management Information Systems. It doesn't matter.

What's important is asking the question: who is the senior individual responsible for thinking about enterprise information technology issues? No organization can survive without a very capable individual acting in this capacity. The title is irrelevant. What is relevant is that this person be entrusted with all of the information processing for the company. Just as the Chief Financial Officer (CFO) is the chief executive in charge of the financial health of the business, the CIO is responsible for the millions of dollars already invested—and the millions more that will be invested—in information technology.

The appointment of a CIO will not alone bring about realignment if the organization did not have it before. The role of CIO was created to bring together all disparate information resources under one chief. It only implicitly addresses some of the business needs by assigning the task of achieving those criteria to a high-level company officer who is linked to the business's goals and concept of success rather than the information technology milieu. However, without changing the relationship and inter-action between the information technology and corporate or-ganization, getting information technology and business aligned is unlikely to be realized.

Let's assume that your organization has a CIO. What are his or her career prospects? With rare exceptions, they frequently can't see themselves becoming business-related executives. They don't aspire to become CEOs. They often see themselves powerless to change that "I" to an "E." For that reason, the tenures of many CIOs are cut short, often to the detriment of their employers. So tenuous is the position of many CIOs, and so short-lived their tenure, that some wags have taken the abbreviation to mean "Career Is Over."

The realignment between corporate and technical manage-ment cannot occur without strong business and technology leadership. The industry needs courageous CIOs who have the vision to harness the pent-up demand for change and focus it in ways that benefit the enterprise. Whatever happens to titles or organizational structures, prospects for individuals with such skills will not be wanting.

If an organization's CIO, or the individual acting in that capacity, does not report to the CEO, the question is, why not? The way information technology fits into the organizational chart speaks volumes about whether information technology is expected to take a reactive or a proactive role. For example, it is hard to reconcile a mandate that information technology must take a strategic, proactive role on an enterprise level, if the CIO reports to a Vice President of Administration.

The CEO-CIO reporting relationship is not a matter of cosmet-ics. Companies in which the CEO and the CIO have close work-ing relationships are typically the first to develop the most sophisticated and powerful business applications. Does your CIO have the flexibility of working in areas that truly impact the strategic direction of the organization? This individual should be working on a handful of top priorities. Here are some points CEOs should keep in mind about the appropriate role of the CIO.

- Someone in the organization must be linking information technology capabilities with the strategic direction of the organization.

- For this linkage to occur, someone who represents information technology must be at the strategic planning table.

- This executive-level individual must address the organization's information challenges strategically—not just set information technology requirements. There's a difference between information systems and information management.

- The CIO should have cross-functional impact. Just as other top executives offer strategic input across many areas of the organization, so should the CIO.

- Avoid overloading the CIO. You should assign the CIO a handful of top priorities.

One clear implication to an aligned CEO-CIO partnership is more CIO participation in strategic planning sessions. Despite the historical limitations of information technology, an enterprise cannot succeed if its CIO is denied access to strategic planning sessions. If a chief executive considers the CIO an expense rather than an asset, he or she is doing both of them a disservice.

[Conversation]

Rapid Change Versus Rabid Change

Frustration is the father of change. When frustration brings about change that only adds frustration, it transforms rapid change into rabid change. When frustration results in meaningful change, it is to be applauded—and so too will be the CEO who brings it about.

Because CIO turnover is among the highest in the business world, with some CIOs lasting only two or three years, many major information technology projects never come to fruition during their initiator's tenure. When another CIO arrives, he or she looks at the situation, declares it not as good as it should be, and makes major changes, which may or may not be fully implemented before the revolving door brings forth yet another CIO.

The effect can be disastrous. Once a company's information technology becomes fragmented and unwieldy, it is likely to be subject to breakdown. When information technology ceases to function smoothly, managers may begin the finger pointing that replaces taking responsibility by assigning guilt. This behavior leads to aimlessness, a kind of throwing up of the hands.

When the frustration level reaches epidemic proportions, the CEO's reaction is often resolute determination once and for all to change the system. At this point the CEO chooses a new CIO, typically from a short list of those who are more than willing to chuck everything out and start again.

---

5. Overcome the Techno-Illiteracy Crisis

Business executives and technical managers must learn to speak the other's language. CEOs must overcome the techno-illiteracy crisis by becoming comfortable with technical terms and concepts. The only reasonable way to accomplish this goal is by actually using the technology to solve business problems. Luckily, as I will show, this is not difficult.

Information technology managers, in turn, must become familiar with elementary business concepts. The only reasonable way to accomplish this goal is by actually using business concepts to solve technology or project management problems. This is not difficult either. But since this is a book about information technology, I will concentrate on the task of acquainting businesspeople with technology and leave for another time the worthy challenge of introducing business concepts to technologists.

[Speech]

Tower of Technobabble

Technologists tend to live in what I call the Tower of Technobabble. We talk about SQL (structured query language, pronounced "sequel"), object-oriented programming (OOP, pronounced "oops"), client/server computing, GUIs (graphical user interfaces, pronounced "gooeys"), neural networks, LANs, WANs, polymorphism, Windows, OS/2, UNIX, and a world of acronyms and alphabet soup.

If you don't have an information technology background, these words sound like gibberish. Or if you relate these terms to conventional knowledge, you come up with something very different. For instance, GUI is what happens when you put a kid together with a hot fudge sundae. Sequel is the second time around for a movie. No one likes to do Windows. UNIX are the neutered slaves that protect harems in old gladiator movies. Polymorphism is some dread disfiguring disease that originated on a South Sea island. And client/server is the oldest profession.

One of the earliest sources of the disconnect between technologists and financial- or marketing-oriented business professionals is the former's predisposition to use technical jargon. Every profession has its acronyms, abbreviations, and buzzwords—indeed, it's one of the qualities that defines a profession—but could there be an industry with a more robust fascination for jargon? When I was last in a Barnes & Noble bookstore, I happened to glance at the shelves dedicated to computers. I was chagrined, but not surprised, to find more than eight dictionaries or glossaries dedicated to information technology. Can anyone explain to me why, though the automobile industry in America is still nominally bigger than the information industry, there were no dictionaries of automobile terminology on the shelf?

Information technologists assume that others of their calling share a common understanding of all the computing acronyms and terms. I don't propose to defend that assumption.

But, indisputably, there are others—significant others—who don't understand: CEOs, presidents, chief operating officers, financial executives. These are the people who run our businesses. These are the people technology is supposed to serve. But they really don't understand the world of information technology or what it is organized to do. They don't understand the basic technology. Even worse, they don't believe it's helping them meet their business goals.

How can this be? To answer this question, let us consider technology from a CEO's perspective.

How does the business professional really see technology? First, it's a huge recurring expense. Second, it's confusing. Third, the promises solemnly made by the managers of information technology have, to an eye-widening degree, not been kept. Fourth, the technology they were told was the answer two years ago is, they are now assured, no longer the answer. Now, the business professional is apprised without a trace of shame, the investments in the existing information technology must be enthusiastically discarded in favor of replacement technology that is in mystery equal to the system in place.

The bottom line is that CEOs and the businesspeople don't understand what technology can do for them. Many of the glowing promises haven't become today's reality. And they don't see technology being applied effectively to their business needs. Recently I read in *The New York Times:* "Most CEOs are asking the question computer managers dread—what is the company getting for all of that money?" Where are the profits? Where is the promised competitive edge?

The message is pretty clear. Technologists must get their heads out of the sand and see the broader picture. Businesspeople cannot tolerate such a myopic view from their colleagues in any area of the enterprise. They have businesses to run and must get the maximum out of any systems they invest in. And they have little use for technologists who are more focused on technology with almost a fanatic religious fervor than they are on helping broaden and improve the businesses they're supposed to serve.

The technologists have a stake in repairing the disconnect. Speaking now as a technologist, I submit that, if we can't speak the language of the businesspeople, then we have no right to expect to be treated as useful contributors. We have a responsibility to translate these technologies, with all their benefits and limitations, into business terms.

[Subway poster]

Techno-illiterate?
We want to help.
Send email to techhelp@nojoke_upyours for information

---

6. Foster an Environment in Which Mistakes Are Welcome

Driving fear out of the workplace is one of the key ingredients of creating a successful work environment. If people are spending hours honing trivia in preparation for a punishing meeting, where is the value for customers? What would happen if those fearful people could work in an atmosphere in which they could safely talk about new ways to serve customers or improve their operations? These are questions asked by Nancy M. Johnson, Vice President for Corporate Research at American Family Mutual Insurance Company. "Unfortunately, there is no way to tabulate the costs for playing head games with employees," she writes, "and there is no way to know what products or services were not invented because people were scrambling to preserve their dignity."

[Anecdote]

Just Don't Do It Again

IBM in the 1950s was the best managed company in the world, thanks largely to the model of the legendary chairman, the senior

Thomas J. Watson. I heard a story about how Watson reacted when he learned about a multimillion dollar mistake made by one of his regional managers. Watson called the sales manager into his office and had words with him. When Watson was done, the hapless manager felt folded, spindled, and mutilated.

"Does this mean you want me to quit?" the manager asked.

"Quit?" replied a sincerely amazed Watson. "Hell no! I just paid more than a million dollars for your education!"

The attitude that no manager has a right to fail is a piece of corporate culture that we will have to discard if we are to repair the disconnect. As Henry Eric Firdman, Director of Strategic Information Systems at Pacific Bell notes, "Information technology is a statistical process and statistics tell us that processes sometimes fail. One of my challenges is to prepare senior management for the potential failures of some systems."

A CEO cannot expect innovative and productive work out of people who are so afraid of making a mistake that they spend an inordinate amount of time covering themselves. At Computer Associates, the most important thing we tell our people is that they have the right to fail. Since they don't have to cover themselves, they are not afraid to make decisions. Decisions come fast and furiously. While a small percentage of them will be mistakes, the company as a whole will be light years ahead of organizations that practice a high-impact choreography of covering up. If employees spend time covering themselves, then they are doing three things wrong: they fail, they waste time, and they deny their colleagues an opportunity to learn from the mistakes. That we won't tolerate.

[Quotation]

People think the CEO has to be the main organizer. No, the CEO is the main disorganizer. Everybody "manages" quite well; whenever anything goes wrong, they take immediate action to make sure

nothing'll go wrong again. The problem is, nothing new will ever
happen again, either.   HARRY QUADRACCI
                                                   CEO, Quad/Graphics

---

7. The Facts Are Friendly: Insist on the Truth

What does commitment to the truth mean? It does not mean
gazing at your naval to find the ultimate meaning of life. It
means, as Peter Senge writes in *The Fifth Discipline*, "a relentless
willingness to root out the ways we limit or deceive ourselves
from seeing what is, and to continually challenge our theories of
why things are the way they are."

There's no way to avoid this particular unpleasant truth: The
exchanges between corporate and technical management at
many organizations have not been entirely truthful. Technical
managers have been guilty of telling their senior managers what
they thought their superiors wanted to hear. Senior managers
have been guilty of accepting such information in the face of
overwhelming reasons for skepticism. Technical managers
didn't want to do the hard work of putting the information in
terms senior managers could understand. Senior managers
didn't want to do the hard work of preparing themselves to
understand the important information. From opposite sides,
both managers were hoping that against all odds the information offered and received would somehow, down the road,
turn out to be defensible. The lying satisfied mutual needs, or
seemed to.

As numerous as the lies are the number of excuses defending
them:

- "There's no way we can do this project in six months, but I
  can't tell my CEO that. Maybe we'll pull off a miracle or
  something."
- "We have to rewrite the application; it's architected wrong."

- "My CEO wouldn't understand the details."
- "My boss can't handle bad news."
- "If I tell the CEO about this mess, he'll shut us down."
- "Lying gets me resources I otherwise wouldn't get."
- "It's a mess, but maybe I can clean it up before the boss finds out."
- "We're too far into the project; it's too late to back out now."

Peter Drucker reminds us that the critical question all knowledge workers must learn to ask is, "What information do I owe?" This, he says, is a difficult question because there is something about the human race that instinctively hoards information. Our first instinct is that what we don't tell isn't going to cause trouble. What we don't tell isn't going to cause change, either.

Let us accept that both sides are guilty and that this practice must stop. The disconnect cannot be repaired without an environment of unhesitating truth and candor. As usual, relief from the culture of deception must start at the top. Senior corporate executives must model truthfulness by being candid with their technology managers. That means sharing strategic information and not pulling back on bad news. That means trusting your information technology managers to handle information with discretion. That means refusing to tolerate being "protected" from bad news, technical or otherwise. That means welcoming the messenger of bad news. And, yes, that means if you don't understand something, admit it.

For their part, technology managers must never again overpromise, overstate, or oversell their capabilities. If they do, they should correct it when they have indications that their promises were unsound. This message must be accepted by every member of the information technology team. Technology managers must also give up the condescending attitude that they are protecting upper management when they withhold information for any reason. Information technology managers must accept complete responsibility for the actions of the information technology resource. Finally, technology managers must learn how to handle sensitive information with discretion if they are to earn the trust of their colleagues.

I offer the position that the facts are always friendly. They may not always be pleasant, but the facts are friendly in the sense that, if they are facts, you are always better off knowing about them than not knowing about them. In the culture of avoiding responsibility that many organizations have spawned, this lesson doesn't swallow easily. There has been too much passing the buck, too much blaming each other, too much condemning Washington or Japan. This observation is not pleasant, but it is a fact, and, like all the other facts bombarding you, I suggest it can be your friend.

[Joke]

No, But If You Hum a Few Bars...

A CEO walks into a psychiatrist's office and says, "My CIO thinks he's a grand piano!"

"Well, bring him in and I'll see what I can do."

"Are you kidding?" the CEO says. "Do you know how much it costs to move a piano?"

[Quotation]

The truth shall set you free but first it shall make you crazy.

ANONYMOUS

[Joke]

Your Mileage Is In, Mr. Muskrat. Have a Nice Flight.

Two information technology managers are talking.

"Did you know that muskrats can fly?" says the first.

"No way," says the second. "Those big ugly rodents can't get off the ground."

"But it's true."

"Give me a break," says the skeptical manager. "How do you know?"

"Well," said the first manager. "The CEO insisted they could."

"Oh," says the second guy very slowly. "Well, sure muskrats can fly, but very low to the ground."

8. Without Trust, Everything Is Friction

My goal is to model confidence in the CIO and every employee. I'm referring, in other words, to trust. And trust, as I hope to show, is the defining feature of an environment where corporate and technical goals are aligned. Attend to what Tom Peters says in *Liberation Management:*

> Trust is essential. Given project autonomy, mutual dependence, contact with outsiders, and work away from "home," an atmosphere of trust is an absolute must—and more of a stumbling block to future organizational success than, say, getting the information technology scheme right.

The type of corporate environment we are striving for is built on unprecedented layers of trust: between corporate and technical management, between the company and its partners, between the company and its customers. Trust must be big enough to welcome mistakes.

[Quotation]

Executives are given subordinates ... they have to earn followers.
JOHN W. GARDNER
American writer and government official, 1912–

[Quotation]
The only way to make a man trustworthy is to trust him.

HENRY STIMSON
American statesman, 1867–1950

9. Rank the Information Technology Managers

At Computer Associates, I have always insisted that managers rank their direct reports. The vast majority of employees have appreciated knowing exactly where they stand. In any team, there will always be a range of aptitudes. The spread of talents is not only obvious, but team members are in remarkable agreement about the distribution. Put any ten people in a room and they will sort themselves out from top to bottom in short order. Organizations that refuse to make these rankings explicit only deny the team management vital information against the day when some adjustments have to be made. That said, my experience in ranking employees suggests two policies:

- Work for the top third.
- Pecking order? OK. Layers? No way!

[Quotation]
He who praises everybody praises nobody.

SAMUEL JOHNSON
British writer, 1709–1794

The Top Third.   Every employee at CA is ranked. It's not a trivial process but, over the years, we have evolved a system that works very well for us. After completing the evaluation process, we let the employees in the top third know only that they have been ranked in the top third. Every other employee is assigned a numerical rank. Computer Associates people are satisfied with this system. For the top third, this system avoids the occasionally counterproductive competition for "number one."

Pecking Order? OK. Layers? No Way! Acknowledge that the pecking order exists but insist that it not be used as an excuse to stifle discussions or lock out people from participating. That means anybody can talk to anybody and that, by and large, people don't worry about rank. Your job is to be conspicuous in seeking out the views of everyone, regardless of where they happen to reside in the hierarchy.

Determining who among your staff is the most valuable contributor is an essential task of any manager. If your CIO has not gone through the exercise of ranking the information technology managers, you must invite him or her to do so. Two benefits will immediately accrue. First, it will become apparent how the rankings of capabilities map to the organization chart of responsibilities. Second, your top rated people, whom you presumably attracted on the basis of your commitment to excellence, will appreciate any exercise that distinguishes between the outstanding and the merely capable.

Ranking employees may seem to go against such management theories as team building, employee empowerment, and other politically correct attitudes, but it is critical to identify the top people in any organization. If you want to structure your organization around performance, it becomes immediately clear that a way must be found to determine which employees perform best. Sure, most companies go through a perfunctory employee evaluation where on a one-to-five scale everyone turns out to be a three. That helps everyone pretend they are equal contributors, but how do you know which threes are the best threes? You don't. At CA, both employees and their managers have much better information for making adjustments when adjustments are needed.

10. Have Fun

The biggest challenge facing tomorrow's managers is finding the outstanding people to do the work. This is doubly true in the information technology field, where the challenge will be to find individuals doubly endowed with first-rate technical skills and keen management instincts. To attract, keep, and motivate a high-quality workforce, companies will have to create an environment of challenge, stimulation, and (dare I say it?) fun.

Somewhere deep in our ancestral memory is buried the notion that work is supposed to be fun. Corporate America has correctly identified this concept as subversive to the rigid, hierarchical organization and has been ruthless in a campaign of zero tolerance for anything approximating fun in the workplace. Yet employees persist in having fun on the job. Some managers suspect that small teams behind closed doors often have fun and don't know what to do when they catch an employee taking giddy delight in the task at hand.

As managers, our job is to optimize for fun. That means creating small teams because spontaneity is impossible in large bureaucracies. That means looking for opportunities to make everyone a winner in some way. That means trusting people. And although optimizing fun is serious business, it means not taking ourselves too seriously.

[Joke]

No Bull: Solve the Right Problem

A reporter is interviewing a bullfighter.

Reporter: "Bullfighting must be physically taxing. How do you exercise to stay in shape for the ardors of bullfighting?"

Matador: "Exercises?"

Reporter: "Yes, you know, jogging or weightlifting to maintain your physical strength."

Matador: "There is something you don't understand, my friend. I do not wrestle the bull."

11
Putting It All Together

Whose problem is this, anyway? The pressure for better alignment is coming from the business units, but the information technology manager or CIO has to engage both the user community and information technology professionals in a partnership effort to assess problems and invent new alignment strategies. By creating the partnership, the CIO should act as a communications bridge between information technology, senior management, and users. But the CIO's most important job is to realign old work values, particularly to legitimize an emphasis on effectiveness versus efficiency and to speed up delivery of new competitive or business-critical systems.

It is also important to remember that information technology does not operate in a vacuum. A couple of anecdotes elsewhere in this section illustrates my point that companies need to align compensation policies, customer service goals, and other elements of the organization with strategic objectives. Adjusting information technology by itself will mean nothing.

Too often, we hear information technology managers say, "Let the users go ahead and do their own systems. They'll come running back when they fail!" When information technology management resists working creatively on the alignment problem, pressure can build and cause an explosion of user and senior management frustration, leaving no time for rational planning and preparation for change.

[Quotation]
Don't be afraid to take a big step if one is indicated.
You can't cross a chasm in two small jumps.
                                                        DAVID LLOYD GEORGE
                                                British statesman, 1863–1945

Furthermore, where are the productivity improvements? Many people are troubled by the productivity statistics released by the Commerce Department and other agencies. Some analysts are troubled because the statistics do not seem to reflect the billions of dollars invested in information technology deployed specifically to raise productivity. Others are worried that these unimpressive rates put the United States at an economic disadvantage relative to other industrialized nations. Others, like me, are troubled by the lack of precision of the statistical process itself. When it comes to measuring the impact of information technology, current statistical processes are woefully inadequate.

According to published statistics, productivity growth in the United States has slowed sharply, dropping from an average of 2.4 percent in the 1950s to 1.3 percent in the 1980s—just when information technology has become pervasive. With the price of computer products dropping dramatically in recent years, companies are buying more computer power, with spending on information technology now accounting for about half of all durable equipment outlays. "You see computers everywhere except in the productivity statistics," notes Nobel laureate and economist Robert M. Solow.

Referring to his study of a sample of large United States and European companies, Professor Gary Loveman of The Harvard Business School says he, "found no evidence of any positive relationship between information technology investment and business performance." While noting that some individual companies have used information technology very successfully, overall productivity gains have been disappointingly small. "For a country that competes in the global marketplace, our productivity rates are a disaster," he says.

I am convinced that, statistics to the contrary, there is, in fact, no productivity paradox. By every measure I apply in my day-to-day activities, I see tremendous impacts on my own productivity as well as the productivity of the people I encounter. This position is supported by a 1994 report called "Information Technology in the Service Society" issued by the National Research Council. For service sector companies, this report refutes the assertions of Dr. Stephen Roach and others that there is no direct link between information technology and productivity. [By the way, Dr. Roach served on the task force, as did AMR's Max Hopper, Kmart's David Carlson, Walter Wriston (late of Citibank), John Opel (late of IBM), and other information technology worthies.]

Other economists are finally expressing the obvious: There is no productivity paradox and there probably never was one. For example, the Fortune 500 companies investigated by MIT Sloan School of Management Economists Erik Brynjolfsson and Lorin Hitt earned an eye-popping 67 percent return after depreciation on their investments in information technology.

Brynjolfsson and Hitt calculated returns on investments in information systems for 367 industrial and service companies from 1987 through 1991. By contrast, the earlier studies that suggested slender productivity gains relied on obsolete data from the 1970s and early 1980s. The large, up-to-date sample revealed the benefits of reorganizing around the new technologies—improved quality and customer service, greater product variety, and time compression in getting products to market. "If there ever was a productivity paradox," says Brynjolfsson, "it disappeared by the late 1980s."

The MIT Sloan School study regards productivity in light of the modern service economy. Managers invest in information

technology to achieve a variety of impacts that have traditionally not been well reflected in industry or macroeconomic
measures of productivity. These new service-oriented measures include:

- *Preserving or expanding market share.* Market share is a key
  measure of competitive success and a basis for gaining relative
  marketing or purchasing power as well as improved economies of scale. To maintain their market share, all companies in
  an industry may be forced to invest in information technology
  even though it does not increase their own output. Thus,
  investments increase, but company or industry volume and
  profits may not.

- *Avoiding risks or alternative costs.* Executives often invest in
  computer systems to avoid risks. The benefits of avoiding
  losses by using better systems are very real to a company, but
  only the costs of achieving them show up in productivity
  measures.

- *Creating flexibility for changing business environments.* Changes
  in the business environment may require unforeseeable
  changes in the way a company operates. As many financial
  services and banking firms have learned, a flexible information technology system may be essential to the very survival
  of the company as it attempts to cope with rapidly changing
  business conditions. In other cases, companies invest in information technology to provide a flexible future platform for
  creating new products that may not yet be planned or even
  conceived.

- *Improving the internal environment.* Firms often invest in
  information technology to provide a greater degree of predictability or stability to their operations. Such investments
  help companies avoid undue fluctuations in sales or profitability. Other firms invest in systems to improve employee
  relations. Properly installed, computers can eliminate tedi-
  ous tasks, make jobs more attractive, or shorten training
  cycles.

- *Improving the quality of products and interactions with customers.*
Companies increasingly compete on their quality of customer service. Computer systems have been especially useful in helping to improve reliability, ensuring more consistent levels of performance and minimizing errors.

That said, information technology people have been less than honest admitting that a number of major investments in information technology have not paid off. There is nothing surprising in this. Investments in machine tools and bridges have occasionally not paid off either. So here's a deal. As a CEO, I'll accept that information technology can improve productivity if CIOs admit when it can't.

In a field so rooted in quantification and precision, Loveman points out that companies don't seem to have ways to accurately reckon their information needs or to review performance. Information resources are not allocated properly because managers don't have a gauge of costs and benefits. This leads to ineffective performance and few, if any, productivity gains.

Despite his severe judgments on the failure of information systems managers, Loveman does not shut the door on the potential of information technology to enhance the performance of organizations. "The capacity of the technology to deliver significant returns is there and has been widely documented for many companies and applications," he writes. The key lies in senior management participating in information technology planning and establishing precise metrics for measuring the performance of information technology.

[Conversation]

The Productivity Paradox

I am convinced that information technology has promoted productivity. I am presented with overwhelming demonstrations of this truth every day. So how do I account for the fact that we see computers everywhere except in the productivity statistics?

I think I have two reasons to explain the discrepancy. First, we simply don't have the metrics. Second, we don't know what productivity really is. Let me use an analogy to explain what I mean. The automobile industry has concentrated billions of dollars on making cars more efficient. Have they succeeded? The answer is not obvious. Yes, the average car gets more miles per gallon of gasoline than it did 30 years ago. But the average car is much smaller and lighter. Yet I believe cars today are orders of magnitude more efficient. This efficiency is not reflected in the mileage statistics because society has found it appropriate to mandate all kinds of environmental constraints on cars. In response, the auto industry developed the catalytic converter and other antipollution devices, all of which impose a performance penalty on the car. The increased efficiency of today's cars has been partially redeemed in cleaner air.

In the same way, I believe the benefits of America's investment in information technology are being redeemed in ways that don't show up in conventional Department of Labor productivity statistics. These benefits include permanent changes in the way people work and play and in the quality of the products and services we consume.

But the biggest benefit was played out on the front pages of the world's newspapers since the fall of the Berlin Wall. Information technology doomed the Soviet system. A large measure of whatever productivity information technology gave us was pledged to ending the Cold War and bringing the former Soviet states to democratic reform. Although there is no way to measure it, no one doubts the investment paid off. For the first time in my memory, Soviet missiles are not targeted on American cities.

There are many ways to calculate the productivity impacts of information technology. Children sleeping sounder is one of them.

[Quotation]

Pick battles big enough to matter, small enough to win.

JONATHAN KOZOL
American author, 1936-

12

Lessons from "The CEO in a Wired World" Conferences

In the months before I started writing this book, I finally noticed just how badly CEOs have been conned. The swindle goes like this: All the CEO has to do to enter the world of tomorrow is to hire a world-class CIO and give him or her a blank check.

It just doesn't work that way.

[Quotation]

Sure the game is rigged,
but if you don't play you can't win.

ROBERT HEINLEIN
American science fiction writer, 1907–1988

In my visits to CA offices around the world, where I have an opportunity to meet with many groups of CEOs, I encountered this perception many times and in many forms. In each case, there was a CEO aloof from the critical issues of information technology. In each case, a true partnership between the CEO and CIO was lacking, resulting in costs that could have been lower, in product time tables that could have been faster, and in customer service satisfaction levels that could have been higher. The individual effects of the disconnect were unambiguous. These encounters redoubled my conviction that for the sake of their organizations in the last decade of the twentieth century, CEOs need to understand the broad issues of information technology and CIOs must understand the broad business issues driving organizations.

I became convinced that a gathering of CEOs in a relaxed setting dedicated to the subject of information technology would be very useful. I suggested that Computer Associates organize a series of conferences for CEOs to explore information technology strategies and to demystify information technology. Although the dynamic I subsequently labeled "the disconnect" was not well formulated in my mind, I was pretty sure that a carefully designed conference could accomplish two important goals:

First, I wanted to put a dent in the incredible level of technophobia displayed by many CEOs. I had a hunch that many CEOs secretly hungered for technical information, even as they argued that they were too busy and that it was somebody else's responsibility.

Second, I wanted to start a productive discussion between CEOs and CIOs. This happy event, I surmised, was eminently feasible, but only after CEOs became a little more familiar with technology.

Thus was born a series of CEO Technology Retreats called "The CEO in a Wired World." Sponsored by Computer Associates and organized by The CEO Institutes (a division of International Media Partners in New York), these retreats aim to empower CEOs to face the challenges of doing business in the global economy. More specifically, the conferences challenge CEOs to begin the difficult task of dismantling the effects of the disconnect and to form a productive partnership with CIOs.

[Quotation]

Twenty years ago, a conference called "The CEO in a Wired World" would not have been possible. Twenty years from now it will not be necessary.   PETER DRUCKER
Business philosopher and author, 1909–

[Quotation]

By 2020, 80 percent of business profits and market value will come from that part of the enterprise that is built around info businesses.   STAN DAVIS and BILL DAVIDSON
Authors, *2020 Vision*

I had no idea whether CEOs would be interested in a headlong nosedive into technobabble. I needn't have worried. Corporate executives can absorb a lot of technology training in a very little time. An impressive number of chief executives have taken the time out of their extremely busy lives to attend. These executives—chairs, presidents, and chief operating officers of some of the largest companies in the world—committed themselves to four rigorous days of hands-on workshops, seminars, program topics, and panel sessions.

The organizers of the first conference seriously *underestimated* how serious the CEOs were. They built in plenty of time for discussion as well as for recreation and soft sessions like a computer golf tournament. The evaluations at the end of the first conference surprised us. The CEOs wanted more, not fewer, hands-on sessions with the hardware and more time, not less, experimenting with the software. This evidence suggests that CEOs are very serious about this subject.

[Quotation]

My function in life was to render clear
what was already blindingly conspicuous.   QUENTIN CRISP
British critic, 1908–

At check-in, delegates to the retreat are issued technology kits including a notebook computer, portable printer, and popular application software for calendaring (scheduling), project management, word processing, and electronic mail. The kit emphasizes connectivity software, including a special CompuServe forum that will permanently link them to other CEOs. Each delegate also receives a CompuServe electronic mail account and $100 worth of services.

Each CEO is also assigned personal technology advisors to accompany them throughout the three days of workshops. This level of one-on-one assistance proves invaluable. The retreat's relaxed atmosphere inspires an easy rapport that encourages CEOs to ask questions and try new skills.

The high ratio of international CEOs attending the conferences surprised me at first. In retrospect, I could have predicted it. The disconnect I describe in this book is an international problem. So it was no surprise that international registration at the conferences typically hovers around 25 percent and occasionally exceeds 33 percent.

In addition to the hands-on workshops, the conference also includes technical presentations, panel discussions, and speakers as illustrious as Peter Drucker, MIT's Nicholas Negroponte, and futurist Alvin Toffler.

The computer literacy of CEOs is usually all over the map. Some delegates have literally never touched a keyboard, while others are comfortable with word processors and electronic mail. But all of the CEOs, regardless of experience, are committed to demystifying information technology and pushing themselves to learn more about it. Some CEOs come with a specific information technology agenda. They want to know more about database technology, say, or networking because their companies are embarking on major database or networking projects. Others have no agenda beyond getting familiar with the technology.

Most CEOs have a dual strategy for attending the retreat. First, they want practice with the technologies that could immediately benefit them in their day-to-day activities. Second, CEOs seek a better understanding of the technology issues and trends that will be needed to prepare their enterprises for the rigors of the twenty-first century.

One of the explicit aims of the conference is to bridge the gulf that has evolved between financial- or marketing-oriented CEOs and their technology-oriented information technology managers. Another objective of the retreat is skill transfer. We do this by taking the CEOs to the edge of the envelope in their understanding of information technology. From the beginning, the conference offers the perspective that the vision for an enterprise's comprehensive information technology strategy must come from the very top. For that reason, CEOs must be as informed about information technology as they are with the myriad other compelling business issues that require their understanding.

After a handful of very successful conferences, I'm confident enough to pass on some of my conclusions and report the observations of some of the CEO participants. The bottom line conclusion is that CEOs acknowledge that they must reengineer their attitudes towards information technology in order to survive in today's increasingly competitive climate. This embrace must be direct, personal, and hands-on.

[Quotation]

No one can be right all of the time,
but it helps to be right most of the time.   ROBERT HALF
U.S. personnel agency executive, 1918–

Delegates to "The CEO in a Wired World" retreat are remarkably forthcoming in their reasons for attending and their hopes for how the retreat will make a difference in their companies. I've followed up on a few of the delegates to the first CEO in a Wired World Conference. Here is a very brief summary of what a few of them said.

Roger N. McMennamy installed a PC in his office five years ago and used it once. That's one time more than other CEOs at the retreat. McMennamy, President and CEO of Cooper Communities, Inc., Bella Vista, Arkansas, a privately held company that specializes in the building of master-planned recreational/retirement communities in Arkansas, Tennessee, and South Carolina, simply couldn't muster either the enthusiasm or time to learn the system.

He decided to attend the retreat because, like other CEOs, McMennamy is determined to model the computer-literate CEO. "In the first two days, I saw specific applications, both strategic and tactical, that I have taken back to my business. I have never used a PC on a regular basis. After seeing what the technology can do, I came away with the objective of making information technology a regular part of my daily regimen," he said.

Cooper Communities is installing a relational database management system that will eliminate the three to six weeks that executives have to wait for certain kinds of sales information:

> My goal is to eliminate the daily hardcopy sales report. Instead, executives should be able to bring up information on their screens and analyze, graph, and perform historical analysis and exception reporting.

Of course, this strategy implies that senior management will have PCs on their desks and not only know how to use the technology but will want to use it. The only way to cause that to happen, McMennamy believes, is to put himself on the line.

Actually, precedent is on his side. A couple of years ago, McMennamy began using the Franklin planner system and offered a companywide seminar on its use. In short order, every member of the senior Cooper Communities management team began using the organizer. McMennamy believes this represents the model for assisting an organization to accept changes: The example has to come from the top down. "You don't have to mandate. If you expect something and set an example that works, people will follow suit. That's what I hope will happen with PC use at Cooper Communities," he told me.

"In retrospect, I regard 'The CEO in a Wired World Conference' as one of the most productive sessions of its type that I've been to," McMennamy concluded. "One of the principal things it has done for me is to let me see how far technology has come. Before the conference, I bought into the mystique that it takes a genius to do the simplest things on computers. Now that I've seen all the things I can do, I'm much less likely to accept statements like 'It can't be done' from information technology."

Let's now hear from Eric Steenburgh, President and CEO of Ricoh Corporation. Ricoh fax machines and copiers are installed all over the world, helping automated businesses in every industry. Yet, as Steenburgh says, the company's executive offices in West Caldwell, New Jersey are seriously underautomated. Moreover, the automation Ricoh has installed is often unintegrated, resulting in people with different systems relying on legitimate but different numbers describing the same processes.

As Steenburgh learned, Ricoh's experience was not an isolated problem. A common symptom of the disconnect is fragmented information systems that report inconsistent results. It drives CEOs to distraction when they cannot be sure which set of numbers to believe. Steenburgh said: "I came to play with the gear. I wanted expertise in software applications. My goal is to go back with enough knowledge to prod my systems people to get everyone to standardize on a common set of applications."

Michael J. Crall, President of Argonaut Insurance Company, a specialty writer of worker's compensation insurance programs, attended to crack another common symptom of the disconnect. "My role is to systematically break down the wall [between the senior management and IT]," he said. "Systems people must be seen as part of the dialogue of the sales process, talking to customers, trying to figure out what they need."

Crall wanted to know what aspects of information technology he needed to understand and, just as important, what he didn't need to jam into his head. "It would be counterproductive for me to get distracted by the details of technology. I want to know what the business requirements are, but I don't need to know what the requirements are vis-à-vis systems I have never seen and never used," he said.

[Quotation]
Keep your friends close, but keep your enemies closer.

SICILIAN PROVERB

While some CEOs primarily resonated to technology strug-
gles internal to their organizations, others looked beyond the
walls of the corporation. "We're being driven by our customers,"
said Ralston Purina's Vice President and Chief Financial Officer,
James R. Elsesser, explaining why every senior executive must
understand issues such as Electronic Data Interchange (EDI).
Elsesser noted that Ralston Purina, manufacturer of products
such as dry dog and cat foods, Wonder bread, and Eveready
batteries must comply with Wal-Mart's policy of "No EDI, no P.O."
In other words, if a company is not prepared to exchange sales and
inventory information electronically, there won't be a purchase
order from the world's most successful retailer. That's a powerful
motivator for understanding EDI. "The answers are out there,"
Elsesser said. "You can't get there by having a dialogue with
yourself."

"The legacy of the last 30 years of information technology has
been largely unfulfilled expectations," said Robert B. Peterson,
Chairman and CEO of Imperial Oil, Ltd. in Toronto, Ontario.
"What's worse is that now information technology actually
represents an obstacle, in many cases, to the critical need for
business process reengineering. I'm here on reconnaissance because we have to do better."

"Information technology is holding us back because the
business planning cycle is so long it takes forever to see the
benefits of change," said George D. Wells, President of Exar
Corporation, San Jose, California. "I want to tell information
technology: We [the company] are the customers; you're the
supplier. If you can't deliver, we'll find someone who can."
Wells insisted that only when information technology can demonstrate success in bringing systems to bear quickly and reliably will it be increasingly invited to participate in the strategic
business decisions of the company.

One of the most stimulating segments of each conference is a panel discussion of CIOs. This no-holds-barred session allows CEOs to understand the constraints CIOs have had to live with. As a result, some CEOs expressed a newfound sympathy for CIOs. On the other hand, the conference made other executives much less tolerant of any obstructionist role their CIOs might take in the future.

The gap between CEOs and information technology took years to develop and will not be bridged overnight. Yet if organizations are to exploit information technology to its maximum potential, the assumptions and objectives of the individuals charged with setting direction for the organization and those charged with deploying information technology solutions must be aligned. After all, two heads—in this case business/financial and technological—are still better than one.

Getting these two heads together won't be easy. I hope conferences like these make a contribution. New organizational approaches such as downsizing and business process reengineering will also help. But CEOs and CIOs must also reengineer their attitudes toward information technology—or abdicate responsibility for increasingly strategic and technically complex business decisions. The first thing we can do is to demystify information technology, to take a look at the technology without the myths or the hype and see what is really of value to our businesses.

I have found it extremely useful to attend every conference. Although they are structured in basically the same way, I find I learn something new from each one. It's an unbelievable privilege to observe CEOs as they learn and work with software. I have come away with powerful insights into product design, documentation, and customer support issues that will make future releases of CA software even better. If one of my public relations managers had come to me three years ago and said, "Charles, I can get a roomful of Fortune 1000 CEOs to sit down, play with our latest software, and give you feedback," I'd have been deeply skeptical. Even if you could get the busiest people in the world to come together for this purpose, I would have asked, how could anyone afford it?

Well, not only do the CEOs come to work with our software, but they pay for the privilege! They are doing it to make themselves stronger managers for their organizations. CEOs want to look at technology for what it is and to decide how to apply it wisely. While they are eager to take advantage of the many benefits of new technology, they also want to hedge their bets in the technology horse race.

The CEOs have found 'The CEO in a Wired World Conference' useful for this purpose. And as they acknowledge the critical importance of information technology to the survival of the enterprise, the CEOs also acknowledge that they need to shape that vision with the help of their CIOs. By the end of the conference, many CEOs find a renewed sense of their mission and specific ideas for helping bridge the gulf that has characterized senior management and information technology.

[Quotation]

Please find me a one-armed CIO so we will
not always hear "on the other hand ..."

CHARLES B. WANG
Chairman and CEO, Computer Associates International,
with apologies to Herbert Hoover

[Conversation]

Rule #1
   Don't sweat the small stuff.
Rule #2
   It's all small stuff.

Part 3
Information Technologies

CEOs must be snowproof. Whether the claptrap comes from a hapless subordinate or the cover story in the latest issue of *Business Week*, they must be able to identify double-talk when they hear it. When it comes to technical information, my observation is that too many CEOs have a difficult time distinguishing the genuine article from the kinds of wholesale nonsense shoveled up by the mythmakers (see Chap. 4) and their ilk. I have seen too many CEOs pounce on half-baked ideas they read about and then make wild extrapolations. A few years ago, *Fortune* published a story about how programming will become so easy that kindergartners will be able to do it. In the next few weeks, more than a few CEOs came to me complaining because their programmers were still having difficulties programming. It became clear to me that too many CEOs could not reliably select between the rich and bewildering variety of technologies available today.

This is technical illiteracy and there's a simple answer for it: information. Because I believe CEOs must have a basic understanding of the various technologies offered, I have selected the technologies that are most likely to figure in any discussion of technological options. While there can be value in each of the options, most have been hyped to the point that their real benefit is obscured. When a technology promises all things to all people, it satisfies few and disappoints many.

My take on these technologies is that, like all tools, they are useful when applied to appropriate tasks. When technologies are considered discredited or unworkable, it is because they have been applied to inappropriate tasks, sometimes shamelessly so. Yet many of these technologies still have their adherents, and CEOs will be exposed to them in any discussion of information strategy. It is better to be prepared.

Many of these topics are recognizable as buzzwords, silver bullets, and panaceas. Each has been celebrated as *the* answer to all of corporate America's woes. Many have made positive contributions. A few have been failures. Most are still not delivering on more than a subset of their promises. None are magic. A passing acquaintance with all is important, if only for self-defense. The topics are:

Computer platforms
  Desktop
  UNIX and open systems
  Midrange
  Mainframe

Database management systems

Graphical user interfaces
  Multimedia

Downsizing and rightsizing

Client/server computing

Network computing

Application development
  Computer-assisted software engineering
  Object-oriented programming

Groupware

Business issues
  Outsourcing
  Business process reengineering
  Quality

[Quotation]

I know all the information technology I need to know ...
if I retire by 3:00 this afternoon.

CHARLES B. WANG
Chairman and CEO, Computer Associates International

13
Computer Platforms

It is no longer business as usual in the data center. Where once the mainframe was master—the unopposed czar of everything in its domain—now midrange workstations, and microprocessors divide authority among all participants. The glass house data centers built for the care and feeding of mainframes are rapidly being augmented by far-flung networks of cooperating machines built by increasingly cooperative vendors. The result? Far more functionality for the computing dollar than ever before. At the same time, the challenges of administering these networks of cooperating devices demand the attention of corporate and technical management alike. The disconnect creates far more problems in the mature environment of distributed computing than it did in the relatively simple world of centralized computing.

The important thing to remember about platforms—the underlying hardware and operating systems—is that they are becoming transparent to the user. It would be wonderful if software applications could run without the cost and practical difficulties of computer platforms. The bargain, however, is that software is useless without platforms to run it, just as a platform has no value if it has no software to run. As long as systems must be delivered on one or more platforms, we must pay attention to their relative merits. I think of hardware platforms as the four worlds of computing:

1. Desktop
2. UNIX and open systems
3. Midrange
4. Mainframe

They are all different, constantly in flux, and dependable only in the certainty that they will change.

[Definition]
Operating System: A collection of system programs that controls the basic operations and functions of a computer. Every computer activity requires the assistance of an operating system. For example, common mainframe operating systems are called MVS and VSE; common operating microprocessor operating systems are DOS, OS/2, and several versions of UNIX.

The landscape of computing in this decade is being formed from the collision of these four different worlds, each with its own limitations and biases. Each world makes a major contribution. Let's take a look at these worlds.

The Desktop

Corporate America has become populated with personal computers of every stripe. Every 18 months, advances in microprocessor technology double the amount of computing power a dollar will buy. Information systems executives, faced with corporate mandates to lower information technology costs, are responding to the call of lower-cost computing. The response is overwhelming the desktops of corporate America and, indeed, the world.

Nine out of ten computing devices sold today are PCs. As powerful by most measures as the mainframes of just a few years ago, PCs will probably dominate every other platform by the end of the century. The most popular type of PCs, with three-quarters of the world market, are compatible with the IBM PC first developed in 1981.

Look for major turmoil in the PC industry. Over 15 years after it was started by a small band of hobbyists, the PC industry is undergoing massive consolidation. The three biggest manufacturers of IBM-compatible PCs today are, according to 1994 figures compiled by Computer Intelligence (La Jolla, California), IBM, Compaq Computer, and Dell Computer. These three now account for about 20 percent of the world market. All these machines depend for their brains on microprocessor chips made by Intel Corp. Apple Computer, whose Macintosh machines are popular in academic applications, uses a Motorola chip and its computers have been incompatible with the IBM standard used in most businesses. Apple is desperately trying to make inroads in the business world, but it is doing so by abandoning the nominally IBM-incompatible status of Macintoshes. The next generation of Macintoshes will essentially be two computers in one chassis: a Motorola-based computer to handle Apple applications and an Intel-based computer to handle IBM applications.

[Conversation]

Ma, Do You Know What Time It Is?

I don't have to tell you that PCs are everywhere. And we don't run into many people anymore who don't know about computers or the technology behind them. Our kids learn programming in school. Computers are used in almost every facet of our lives. In our cars. In our dishwashers. In our coffee pots. Even my mother, who is 76 years old, has her own PC and she loves working with

Windows. Nor does she hesitate to call me, even in the middle of the night, with advice on some new software product.

The success of personal computing can be explained by emphasis on the first term first. PCs took off because people quickly saw how quickly they could be used on a personal basis. No doubt the economics of personal computing also contributed to their success, but the human attraction dominated, and still does. Every PC innovation that has survived (the graphical user interface, the mouse pointing device) helped create a productive relationship between people and the machine. Every innovation that has gone by the wayside proved to be an obstacle.

So organizations went hog wild installing PCs, no doubt with tremendous boosts in productivity. The downside, however, was a conglomeration of desktop devices assembled without rhyme or reason. These systems, designed to address individual or departmental requirements, quickly demonstrated their fragility. Installed without the customary centralized disciplines that ensured data integrity, backup, and security, these systems quickly created difficulties for their users. One problem was especially frustrating. The PC revolution created a base of increasingly sophisticated knowledge workers eager to mine the value from the wealth of corporate information collected by the enterprise over the years. Until recently, easy access to this data was a real problem. A secondary issue was connecting the PC systems to each other, enabling true resource sharing and group computing. Fortunately, both of these issues, as I will show later in this section, have been addressed.

[Anecdote]

Well, the Computer Is Allowing Us to Wait Much Faster!

A large soft drink bottling company thought it identified an opportunity to save money and decrease errors by using laptop PCs. It noticed that company truck drivers were idle as their trucks were being loaded and unloaded. Moreover, the delivery records, which were maintained manually by warehouse people, often took three or four days to get to headquarters where they would be keyed into the computer. Errors would invariably creep in.

The CIO and his team went to work. Why not equip the drivers with laptop computers? While the trucks were being loaded and unloaded, the drivers could enter the data and instantly update the central computer by electronic messaging. The system seemed perfect: a sequential process replaced by a parallel process, one-time entry of shipping records, electronic data interchange, time compression. The company calculated it would save three hours per driver per day.

The system was installed, it seemed to work as intended, but the projected time savings did not materialize. The soft drink trucks took as much time as ever to load and unload. Perplexed, the company brought in a consultant to investigate the situation and recommend modifications. Perhaps the laptop was the problem or maybe it was the communications software.

The consultant observed the truck drivers for a day, made one call to human resources, and explained the situation this way: There was nothing wrong with the technology. It was simply that the truck drivers were paid by the hour. For every hour they finished early, they received an hour's less wages. They had a powerful negative incentive to use the system. The consultant suggested a way to share the savings with the drivers. Immediately, the company saw the productivity benefits it had originally anticipated.

I am indebted to SHAKU ATRE
Atre Associates, Inc., Port Chester, New York for this anecdote.

UNIX and Open Systems

UNIX has been at the forefront of the standards movement. Even though the standards organizations have not yet succeeded in developing a standard UNIX, they have raised everyone's awareness of the need to interoperate and to port applications, which is the ultimate benefit of open systems. Although there are many different flavors of UNIX from many different vendors, it is still easier to port applications to different UNIX systems—and connect them—than it is among any other environments.

UNIX systems are also tremendously scalable. In other words, it is relatively easy to add processing power across a broad spectrum of requirements with minimal cost and effort. As a result, enterprises can start small and add to their UNIX systems as their needs emerge, confident that their entire investment is well protected.

It is easy, then, to see why so many organizations are considering UNIX as the target environment for their mission-critical applications. We have UNIX on midrange environments as well as on the desktop. And now, we have UNIX systems that rival the mainframe in power and capacity. The price/performance ratio of UNIX is very attractive for a large number of applications. For the same amount of power, a UNIX system is far less expensive than a mainframe environment of the same size.

Still, there is one thorny downside. As in the PC world, enterprises building UNIX systems miss the robust systems management capabilities they have come to expect in mainframe-based mission-critical environments. I'm talking about tools like automatic tape backup so that they don't have to worry when files are lost or damaged, policy-based security so that they don't have to protect a file every time one is created, job scheduling so that they don't have to manually sequence the jobs they run, tape protection so that they don't have to worry about tapes being overwritten, and so on. Companies are reluctant to move serious processing to this world without these controls, an area that Computer Associates is helping business address.

Midrange

The third world is typified by special computers that occupy the tier between the largest mainframes and standalone desktop devices. These machines don't fit neatly into the other categories, but nonetheless are providing "bet-your-business" environments for thousands of companies.

These environments are very attractive because they are the closest thing to turnkey processing we have in the industry. They are extremely popular for departmental processing. And many small businesses are using them for their entire operation.

At one time, before networked PCs promised unlimited performance, midrange computers (also known as minicomputers) served a legitimate need. They did the job for small companies or departmental business groups that could not justify the expense of a mainframe computer yet had substantial business needs such as accounts receivable or inventory management. Companies like Digital Equipment Corp., Hewlett-Packard, and IBM dominated this market by supplying systems generally in the $50,000 to $750,000 range.

The popularity of the standalone, proprietary midrange computer, however, is threatened by increasingly powerful networks of PCs and workstations. The economics of microprocessors is simply too overwhelming for midrange systems to combat. Digital Equipment Corp., which helped create the midrange market in the early 1970s, has lost its dominant position in this market. Other midrange manufacturers such as Wang Laboratories, Data General, NCR, and Prime Computer are either bankrupt, acquired, serving increasingly niche markets, or have moved toward UNIX as their primary offering.

The optimum role for midrange computers is to become open to client/server processing as powerful enterprise information servers. IBM's strategy is proving this point. Because of the limitations of languages supported and lack of open interfaces, IBM's AS/400 midrange system had traditionally been a standalone machine. This has limited its effectiveness in participating in distributed and client/server computing. IBM made some changes and created a true success story. Chances are better than even that an AS/400 is toiling somewhere in your organization.

IBM's incredible success with the AS/400, introduced in 1988, suggests that there is still life in the midrange market. Within five years, IBM had sold over 250,000 units, contributing over $14 billion in revenues (and, more important, $2 billion in profits) to the company's beleaguered bottom line, according to the company's 1993 annual report.

Much of the past success of the AS/400 has been based on its ability to adapt rapidly to changes in the market. The 1993 AS/400s are very different from those first announced in 1988, which is a credit to IBM, a company not previously appreciated for being fast on its feet. While the 1993 models of the AS/400 will run any applications written for the older machines, there have been dramatic changes in capacity, cost, openness, and the ability to connect PCs as workstations. In the next few years, IBM will announce changes in the operating system that will further blur the distinction between AS/400s and the PCs and workstations to which they are increasingly connected. So the AS/400 has succeeded precisely to the extent that IBM has relaxed the system's proprietary midrange uniqueness and hitched it to the growth of network computing.

[Anecdote]

Give Me a Pound of Software to Go

People often ask me to show them the software we create. It's an impossible request because software itself is an abstraction. At the risk of aging myself, I offer the following anecdote as an example of the difficulties encountered when we try to pin software down.

Back in the days of NASA's Mercury project, every launch had a Weight Control Officer whose job it was to carefully weigh every item going into the space capsule. One day the Weight Control Officer strolls into the data center and wants to know the exact weight of the software going up with the next launch.

"Software is weightless," reply the programmers.

The Weight Control Officer is skeptical. His experience is every-thing weighs something. So he investigates.

Now remember, this is the early 1960s when programmers used stacks of punch cards to run computers. The next day, he runs back into the data center holding a big stack of punch cards. "Can't fool me!" he yells. "Software does too have weight. The launch control program weighs exactly 32.35 ounces!" He holds one of the cards up to the light, the better to see the dozens of keypunch holes in the card. "How can you tell me that software is weightless?"

The programmers look at the Weight Control Officer with pity.

"Software is weightless," they respond, "because we use only the holes."

Mainframe

Is the mainframe computer dead? Not in this lifetime. American businesses have invested billions of dollars in programs that have defined and changed economic and social life in the last decade of the twentieth century. The mainframe computer has been—and remains—an inexorable part of the fabric of our culture. Still, these are the inescapable facts:

- The mainframe market is shrinking by almost 10 percent every year.

- At the same time, there has been a net increase in mainframe processing power.

- Mainframe manufacturers are all diversifying into other plat-forms to counteract the lost revenues from mainframe sales.

- Amdahl and Fujitsu, the two largest mainframe manufacturers after IBM, have agreed to trim manufacturing and R&D expenses by jointly developing their next generation of mainframes.

- IBM has recently announced a new mainframe pricing policy that would have been considered heresy only a year ago: All mainframe prices are now completely negotiable.

The race may not always go to the swift,
nor the battle to the strong, but that's the way to bet.

ANONYMOUS

The mainframe is the home of what the industry pundits like to call "legacy systems." But these are the systems that drive our businesses today. Over the past 30 years, American business has made huge investments in software and, more importantly, in the people building and maintaining these systems. The reality is that it is a sound business practice to protect and leverage investments, not abandon them.

This is probably the greatest reason why, contrary to popular belief, the mainframe is not dead. Nor is its demise imminent. Why do so many businesses still rely so heavily on the mainframe? Because it's a proven environment. It is highly reliable and secure. It still delivers the highest performance on I/O of any environment. And it has the most robust online transaction processing environment available. But the role of the mainframe in computing is changing. While the mainframe will probably continue to churn out back office systems, it will most likely become the corporate server or information factory of the next decade.

Yet there's no dearth of news about the death of the mainframe. Unit sales are decreasing while unit prices are dropping. A recent survey by Forrester Research, Inc. found that 20 percent of the 1000 largest U. S. companies see "no future" for their mainframes. These firms represent the mainframe's biggest market. Realistically, mainframes will have to yield most of their services to PCs and workstations.

That said, many of the problems for which mainframes were designed are getting more—not less—complicated. The volumes of data to be manipulated grow exponentially. People's demand for up-to-the-second information is insatiable. Everyone wants service, and they want it faster, cheaper, more reliably, and more securely than ever before. When it comes to large amounts of information that has to be processed quickly, reliably, and securely, mainframes still represent the best and sometimes only technology to do the job.

Of course, it's not the mainframe that's important. It's the power of the mainframe—the functionality that businesspeople can exploit to solve business problems—that's at issue. In this sense, a mainframe is better seen as a process than as a piece of hardware. As the process changes, the hardware inexorably will too. The old architecture of the mainframe was designed to talk to lots of people by not working very closely with any of them. This orientation has to change because business conditions have changed.

Some of the tasks required of mainframes in the past can be done better and more cheaply by PCs. That's good, because rightsizing or shifting workloads to the most efficient processing platform is good for business. Modern business practice calls for decentralized systems: bringing information processing as close to the end user or customer as possible. That's good, because quality improves when the distance between customers and those who serve them decreases. As a result, a lot of work formerly done by mainframes has been offloaded to networked PCs and midrange computers.

But don't unplug the mainframe. There will continue to be a range of problems that only mainframes can handle. The mainframe, in whatever guise it may appear, remains our best assurance that the exchange of information is orderly, secure, and error-free.

[Quotation]

If Aetna Life & Casualty today took away the computers—those mainframes that people talk about being dinosaurs—there'd be no company there. You'd have to have all the people on the East Coast processing transactions to handle the business of the West Coast.

IRWIN J. SITKIN
Former Vice President of Corporate Administration,
Aetna Life & Casualty Co.

[Conversation]

What Goes Around Comes Around

When mainframes were first introduced commercially in the 1950s, many pundits were decidedly skeptical. They thought that the computational problems mainframes were designed to address applied to maybe five or six organizations in the country, maybe the Strategic Air Command or the Census Bureau. But for the vast majority of businesses, mainframes represented a solution looking for a problem. In the early 1950s, IBM Chairman Thomas J. Watson predicted the total worldwide market for mainframes at about 25 units.

He couldn't have been more wrong, of course. Over the next 40 years, virtually every enterprise worthy of the name installed a mainframe computer. It's hard, in retrospect, to imagine the business environment without centralized, mainframe computers anchoring our largest organizations, maintaining repositories of the information that increasingly drive our lives.

Why did thousands of organizations spend individual sums in the tens of millions of dollars on these machines? It wasn't out of a sense of adventure or desire to explore the limits of computing science. Without exception, mainframe computer systems were purchased by flint-hearted executives who were convinced the machines represented the best alternative for solving their pressing business problems. If they had concluded that armies of gerbils with green eyeshades could do the job better, then the best selling item in company cafeterias across the country would be Purina gerbil chow.

These executives put their money in mainframe technology because mainframes demonstrably addressed a larger number of pressing business problems than they created. Virtually singlehandedly, the mainframe computing environment created the information-based, online world on which we have come to rely. Without mainframes, none of the applications we use every day—the telephone network, automated teller machines, satellite television, airline reservation systems, overnight delivery services— would be possible.

These four worlds of computing are coming together. It is a natural union because the weaknesses of each world are compensated by the strengths of the others. We have the end user empowerment of the PC world, the openness and scalability of UNIX, the model for turnkey processing exemplified by the AS/400 midrange system, and the robustness and mission-critical capability of the mainframe. When they all come together we see a robust client/server environment for mission-critical processing. And this is the world that we are moving toward—a world of mixed environments where you are free to choose how you will implement systems to best serve your business.

[Conversation]

Seven Lessons from the Glass House

I grew up in the glass-walled mainframe data center, and the skills I learned have stood me in good stead. What's more, as Computer Associates helps create the world of distributed, decentralized computing, these skills from my mainframe days have been constantly valuable. The seven lessons are:

1. *Standards.* Establish and enforce standards for the way resources are named, applications written, and user authorizations set up.

2. *Discipline.* Establish lines of communication among the people administering the various PC networks.

3. *Security.* Establish and enforce corporate security policies, keep sensitive data on the most secure platforms, audit the system for security weak spots, and define and disseminate new security practices such as password control schemes, data encryption, or user identification systems.

4. *Software license accountability.* Enforce adherence to software licenses by monitoring systems for unauthorized copies of software.

5. *Documentation*. Document the overall network configuration, distribute it to all PC managers, and update it regularly.

6. *Data backup.* Enforce regular backup of all server data.

7. *Data integrity.* Establish corporate data models to avoid redundancies in personal and departmental databases.

14

Database Management Systems

The Egyptians managed the data about the pyramids on clay tablets. On knotted ropes, the Aztecs, no doubt, stored inventories of virgins to be sacrificed. Modern libraries developed the card catalog. In the 1950s, college Romeos carried little black books while corporate executives maintained Rolodexes. Executives today manage names and phone numbers in personal digital assistants. Every society evolves database management systems (DBMSs) to meet its requirements.

The requirements are remarkably similar. The role of every DBMS in history has been to logically store data so that it can be quickly and easily accessed. This is no less true today, although the volumes of data to be managed have never been greater nor the stakes higher. More than any time in human history, the ability to efficiently find and process data into information for day-to-day business decisions is of paramount importance. More and more, the ability to create new information-driven products and services rapidly is separating the winning companies from the losers.

Over the past 20 years, the subject of database access has generated more mystery than any technology I know. Despite that, people cling to their databases with almost religious fervor. To meet the emerging database management needs of modern corporations, information technology developed a number of DBMS architectures. All these architectures organize and access data differently, but all have the same goal: to allow the database user to find specific information quickly and accurately. The main architectures are:

Navigational systems. The first DBMSs ran on mainframe computers and stored records in a long list or hierarchy. For example, a telephone directory is a hierarchical DBMS, with the alphabet determining the order. When a piece of information is requested, the computer searches through the file until it finds the requested record. This is the most efficient method of accessing data. However, the technique used by programmers is not all that simple or straightforward.

Relational systems. Relational database management systems (RDBMS) use a tabular or matrix architecture designed to simplify access to data by programmers. The data are grouped into tables with rows and columns that have a relationship to each other. In a relational directory assistance system, operators can search by subscriber name, street address, or phone number and bring up the appropriate record. This is possible because the RDBMS stores not only the data elements (name, address, and phone number) but the relationships between the data elements as well.

In the last 10 years, relational systems have clearly dominated the market. The reasons are numerous. With modern, high-speed computers, relational systems perform nearly as well as hierarchical systems. But most important, a clear standard for defining and accessing relational data has emerged. Thanks to IBM's Structured Query Language (SQL), relational systems developed by many vendors (including Computer Associates) can talk to each other and access common databases. SQL has formed the basis for compatibility of database systems across numerous environments.

The systems that are driving our businesses today—the so-called legacy systems—were built mostly with COBOL and navigational databases. In the early 1980s, relational technology dominated the headlines and there was a great deal of noise over the use of SQL. The good news was that SQL was, and still is, a very powerful tool for ad hoc query and decision support. The bad news was that proponents insisted that SQL could and should replace the established navigational tools. Remember, the revolutionaries feel they must destroy the old in order for the new to succeed.

After ten years, we are finally beginning to see SQL used in mission-critical applications. But, oddly enough, it has not replaced the prior systems, and it is still most successful in query and decision support applications. Now, relational is old hat and everyone is talking about object-oriented programming. This type of approach is great for programming that takes advantage of the new graphical user interfaces (GUIs). There is even noise about new object-oriented databases which, of course, will replace the relational databases, or worse still, will sit side-by-side with your existing databases. Is it really feasible to expect that we will have to retain navigational databases and relational databases and object-oriented databases, possibly all containing the same information? Of course not. Yet that is what FUDGE (see Chap. 5) holds out unless we are careful.

[Interview]

Just-in-Time Information

Charles, how do we ferret out the pieces of information that are most critical and provide that information to the right person at the right time to do the right job?
You've heard of just-in-time manufacturing?

Sure. Just-in-time ensures that exactly the parts needed for a manufacturing process are available at just the right time, neither earlier nor later, and at just the right place.

Well, just-in-time information ensures that decision makers get exactly the information they need at just the right time, neither earlier nor later, and at just the right place.

What's required for JIT information?

A materials tracking system is a prerequisite for companies being able to implement JIT in its traditional sense. You had to know where everything was in order to get it where it was supposed to be at the right time. I also believe that it's a key discriminator in the companies who are going to be able to deliver JIT information. In this case, what's required is a distributed database management system that keeps track of the components of the total information asset located in remote sites, who is responsible for keeping that information valid, and the requirements for being able to access it.

15
Graphical User Interface (GUI)

Computers are really only good at adding ones and zeros very quickly. The designers of the first computers, therefore, didn't put much thought into the user interface—the way the computer presents itself and its results to its human masters. If the early computer specialists programmed the machines to present any kind of user feedback, it was usually terse and cryptic, using codes more often than English. If any of the early designers thought about making the user interface less hostile, the disconnect operated to dissuade them. After all, computers wouldn't be so mysterious and deserving of all that programming support if common people understood what a computer reported after it chewed up their job.

One of the most powerful benefits of the personal computer is the development of the graphical user interface, known affectionately by the acronym GUI and even more affectionately pronounced "gooey." The GUI front end to computers, dominated by Microsoft Windows, has all but replaced the old alphanumeric character user interface.

Popularized by the Apple Macintosh, the GUI screen allows novice computer users to be more productive. GUI applications allow users to manipulate information and launch applications through the use of icons on the screen. The use of a mouse pointing device allows users to move away from the keyboard, making the computer much easier to use for those who have not learned to type. Users can perform activities on the computer simply by pointing to them. Chunks of information, as well as images, can be captured and moved from application to application simply by dragging and dropping them from one location to another.

It is unlikely that computers would have become so widely used had a GUI standard not been developed and marketed so well by Microsoft and others. The GUI standard uses the metaphor of a window to represent information on a screen. Each application or document is represented by a window on the display screen. Multiple windows can be opened at one time, allowing users to work on several documents or applications at once. All GUI applications have similar tools such as pull-down menus, dialogue boxes, and consistent navigation techniques. Software developers now work for a consistent "look and feel" for business applications. The "look" involves the objective appearance of each application. The "feel" refers to the mysterious but critical interaction between the user and the computer application.

This consistency between GUI-based applications makes all the difference. For the first time, users who learn one GUI application can quickly learn another one based on the same user interface. A consistent user interface minimizes training expenses for the user and software support costs for the vendor. Industry studies have found that a GUI can double or even triple productivity over a character-based interface.

[Joke]

"Humor Missing—Joke Aborted"

A well-known consultant in the field of user interface design has a logical hobby: She collects computer error messages. In the early days of computing, messages such as "illegal entry," "fatal input error," and "parameter missing—job aborted" were common.

These messages were from techies to techies, so they lacked a certain—how shall I say it—diplomacy. But some error messages were particularly hostile or useless. I asked her to share her favorites (comments are hers):

- "Existential Error." *(I take it back. I regret wishing you didn't exist.)*
- "System frozen by user request." *(I'm sure I must have had a good reason for it.)*
- "This error should not occur." *(Then why did you allow it to?)*
- "Expression too complex." *(Was I frowning at you?)*
- "First time for this disk." *(I didn't know. I'll be gentle.)*

My personal favorite is the error message that the computer of a petroleum company in Houston spits out when corrupted data gets into the system [twangy Texas drawl mandatory]: "Shut 'er down, Clancey, she's spewin' up mud!"

I am indebted to DR. SUSAN WEINSHENK
Weinshenk Consulting, Edgar, Minnesota, for these items.

Multimedia

Multimedia, one of the hottest buzzwords in the industry for the last few years, is just a fancy name for something that combines the capabilities of technologies that used to be separate. Multimedia simply mixes into the PC the functions of these components, combining elements like text, graphics, sounds, and still or motion pictures in a smooth way to present training or information.

[Definition]

Multimedia: Robust applications full of color images, video and sound. A computer system capable of seamlessly manipulating data in several formats (such as text, graphics, sound, and still or motion video) and allowing navigation and presentation of the data formats.

Video conferencing is one of the most popular applications enabled by multimedia. For a growing number of sophisticated companies, especially those operating internationally, television is moving from the employee lounge to the conference room. In doing so, television, the most pervasive and influential medium in the history of the world, is taking its rightful place in the tool kit that companies have for communicating with their employees, customers, suppliers, and other groups.

After false-starting in the early 1970s, video conferencing will become a major factor in the next five years. Sales of video systems are expected to leap from $660 million in 1993 to $10.8 billion in 1997, according to Personal Technology Research, Waltham, Massachusetts. Reason? Reduced equipment costs and sharper pictures make video conferencing the next best thing to being there. Desktop systems ranging from $3500 to $10,000 are already on the market. The boom in higher bandwidth networks will soon enable very low-cost transfer of voice, data, and live video images. Whether as a tool for marketing, training, project management, or public relations, video conferencing will be a major force in the late 1990s.

[Quotation]

Don't write anything you can phone, don't phone anything you can talk face to face, don't talk anything you can smile, don't smile anything you can wink, and don't wink anything you can nod.

EARL LONG
Louisiana politician, 1895–1960

16

Downsizing and Rightsizing

[Definition]

Downsizing: The activity of moving an application, often a mission-critical application, from mainframes to smaller, more efficient computer platforms (*see* Rightsizing).

[Definition]

Rightsizing: The activity of moving an application from its traditional computing platform to one best suited to the task being performed. The target platform is often but not always physically smaller than the existing platform (*see* Downsizing).

While most people agree on what a downsized application is, a standard definition of the term *downsizing* is still emerging. *Downsizing* is often a confusing term to some users, given that downsized systems often seemed bigger, faster, and more powerful than the upsized systems they replaced. Another term frequently used is *rightsizing*, a euphemism that recognizes the fact that budgets and headcounts as well as systems can be downsized. In England, the preferred term is *descaling*. At least one unfortunate data center manager attributed his recent unemployment to what he bitterly labeled, "Hit-you-upside-the-head-sizing."

The point is that downsizing, by whatever name, means changes, economic upheavals, and a certain amount of chaos. Organizations that have an appetite for cost savings, are tolerant of a little chaos, and are willing to accept a certain amount of risk will benefit most. Data center staffs and systems developers need to recognize that, like it or not, downsizing represents the new face of information technology. Collectively and individually, those who are not willing to participate will be left behind. Fortunately, client/server architectures (discussed in the next chapter) create opportunities that organizations and individuals, if they are prepared, can exploit.

In functional terms, downsizing involves moving applications from mainframes to smaller platforms, often client/server database computing architectures. It is a very powerful evolutionary trend. According to a 1993 Dataquest study, 80 percent of mainframe users are investigating downsizing. On the other hand, only a small percentage of those considering downsizing have actually committed to the costly and disruptive process of migrating from one platform to another.

Downsizing is to mainframes what the ubiquitous Vegomatic—as seen on late night television commercials—is to tomatoes. Downsizing slices and dices the mainframe. It carves up the power and functionality normally trapped inside the costly behemoth and parcels them out to a network of dozens or even thousands of small computers.

Nobody downsizes for its own sake. Downsizing offers an enterprise specific benefits ranging from cut-and-dried dollar savings to strategic considerations that force a fundamental change in the way business is conducted. The main benefits of downsizing can be summed up as productivity, flexibility, timeliness, and cost savings.

[Quotation]
First we will be best, and then we will be first.

GRANT TINKER
American television executive, 1926–

Anyone who has used a desktop system for personal productivity, for development or as an intelligent workstation intuitively knows the benefits. The power of graphical user interfaces and the consistency of response time result in dramatic improvements in *productivity*.

The *flexibility* of being able to choose the right systems for the right job and the right workload allows organizations to grow incrementally. Rather than paying for large jumps in power when we outgrow our current systems, we can grow gradually and always keep capabilities close to our current need.

The *timeliness* of developing and deploying downsized systems may represent their ultimate benefit. At a time when the prime requisite for success is being first with information, the market favors organizations that can focus their resources flexibly and develop information technology quickly. Downsized systems are inherently quicker to develop and easier to modify than their host-based counterparts.

The *cost savings* of downsizing are celebrated but by no means clear-cut. While the upfront equipment costs of downsized systems may be low relative to mainframe implementations, hardware only accounts for about a third of the total cost of computing. Over a five-year period, calculates the Meta Group, a Westport, Connecticut-based consulting firm, the operating costs (excluding hardware) of PCs on LANs is actually higher ($15,000) than corresponding applications on mainframes ($10,200).

[Conversation]

Out with the Old, In with the New

Only five years ago, the Computer Associates data center seemed to stretch out for miles. There seemed to be thousands of blue boxes. The incredible part is that it held a total of 72 MIPS in several mainframe systems which today is still a pretty powerful mainframe environment. We never would have dreamed of having that kind of power in a small system.

And despite the attempts of the industry gurus to obscure the issues, the technologies that make this possible are not that complex. The term *downsizing* simply means the ability to move or augment applications from larger systems to smaller, seemingly more cost-effective systems. The client/server architecture separates application processing on one system from the database that resides on another system. And this is just the first step toward more distributed processing technologies, such as a distributed database that spreads the database across several computers.

The technology exists today to allow us to implement these different forms of distributed processing and downsizing. And it's no accident that Computer Associates has pioneered much of that technology. But with a difference. I believe that there is no value in these new technologies if you have to throw your legacy systems away.

And don't trust anyone who says, "We have to rewrite it, because it's architected wrong." They are being lured to the rocks by the sirens of new technology. There is tremendous value in building on the investments in technology and know-how that have already been made.

[Quotation]

If you become familiar with downsizing, you may avoid the task of becoming familiar with outsourcing.   Dr. GEORGE SCHUSSEL
President, Digital Consulting, Inc.

17

Client/Server Computing

[Definition]

Client/Server Computing: Computing that divides information processing between one computer that requests a service and another that performs the function on a machine best suited to perform it.

There's one main point I want you to keep in mind as we talk about client/server computing: When any magical, new technology promises you benefits if only you abandon your investment in existing technology, keep looking. The magic is only in its ability to make your dollars disappear.

The headlong rush into client/server computing has changed the information systems landscape so dramatically in the past five years that it is hardly recognizable. Who would have guessed in 1988, for example, that using many networked PCs and workstations can deliver more computing horsepower at lower hardware prices than using one large centralized system?

Even as little as two years ago, skeptics groused that, sure, client/server systems may have their place for specific, low-impact applications, but they would never be ready for prime-time. Client/server applications, that is, would never be reliable and robust enough to be entrusted with a company's mission-critical business applications. Technologists who cut their teeth manhandling mainframe computers resisted the new informa-tion development and information processing paradigms man-dated by the client/server methodology.

That was then, this is now. A lot of client/server code has been written since the acceptance of the PC and workstation in cor-porate environments. Today, client/server systems are begin-ning to run some of the most demanding applications that businesses have developed.

[Quotation]

Any technology sufficiently advanced is indistinguishable from magic.

ARTHUR C. CLARKE
British science fiction writer, 1917–

The question is not if client/server implementations will take over, but when. No other area of technology will grow faster or hold the interest of executives longer. This is not a totally happy development. Users rushing to reap the anticipated cost savings of client/server computing will almost certainly be disap-pointed when they factor in extra costs for software, manage-ment, training, and other hidden costs.

Nevertheless, client/server systems will account for nearly half of the development resources of major companies by the end of the decade, according to Forrester Research, Inc., Cam-bridge, Massachusetts. This statistic reflects a dramatic change in the way companies use computers, from today's monolithic timesharing systems, typified by dumb terminals attached to a central host processor, to client/server systems that distribute processing across networked computers.

Does this mean the mainframe and large midrange platforms are dead? Not at all. They will play a role in client/server systems as heavy-duty information repositories and servers. Mainframes may well become the information warehouses of the future.

But here is a caution: If your CIO tells you that rearchitecting all your systems to client/server will save money, be skeptical. Everything I've seen suggests that the total costs of client/server computing—hardware, software, conversion of existing systems, development of new systems, training, management— will be higher than the costs of mainframe computing.

Client/server empowers the end user. With improved desktop tools, users at all levels now take on the attributes of true knowledge workers instead of simply data entry clerks. Putting the necessary graphics and processing power into the hands of knowledge workers can do wonders for a business, enabling users to leverage the information assets of the company to be more competitive. Virtually all development work in the future will be done on GUI-based workstations and PCs.

Modern applications have become so complex that users demand a simplified user interface using a graphical front end. Rather than accept a simple text-based screen-at-a-time presentation, users want to interact with a knowledge base through icons, graphics, pictures, and video in an intuitive style. They expect all this and with subsecond response time too. Such capabilities demand some intelligence built into the terminal and a different architecture to manage the new relationships between computer and user. That means a client/server approach.

The cultural issues of client/server computing are every bit as compelling as the technical issues. As organizations evolve away from a centralized computing environment, a new way of thinking about systems is required. A client/server architecture consists of a client process and a server process that are distinct, that typically operate on separate computer platforms, yet that operate seamlessly. In a client/server environment, the lines between traditional mainframe, midrange computer, and workstation capabilities are often irrelevant. Programmers can no longer take a holistic approach, but rather must split the functionality between the client and server, consciously thinking of the role of each. This can be a major culture shock to experienced mainframe programmers.

[Joke]

Are You Sure It Isn't the Other Way?

Having a hard time telling mainframe and client/server computing apart? Here's a clue:

- Mainframe computing is a system of information processing in which workers torment their fellow workers.
- Under client/server computing, the reverse is true.

[Joke]

Top Ten Reasons Client/Server is Like Teenage Sex

10. It's on everybody's mind all the time.

9. Everyone is talking about it all the time.

8. Everyone thinks everyone is doing it.

7. Almost no one is really doing it.

6. Everyone is concerned about the size of their components.

5. The few who are doing it are doing it poorly.

4. The few who are doing it are sure it will be better next time.

3. The few who are doing it are not practicing it safely.

2. Most problems can be traced to the connectors.

1. Everyone is bragging about their successes all the time, although few have actually had any success.

I am indebted to DR. HOWARD RUBIN
Pound Ridge, New York for this list.

[Quotation]

If at first you don't succeed, you'll get a lot of free advice from people who didn't succeed either.

CHARLES B. WANG
Chairman and CEO, Computer Associates International

18
Network Computing

Network computing makes it possible for users to access a wide spectrum of information, applications, and computing resources without worrying about where they are located or how they are connected. While this is an ideal and we still have a ways to go before instant, transparent access to information is a widespread reality, network computing has given millions of users unprecedented access to information. It has also expanded the vision of organizations, allowing enterprises to look outward to customers and suppliers who can, for the first time, participate in the network. It's also the underlying technology for client/server computing. Network computing reflects the way most modern organizations work.

In the past, most organizations had no choice but to standardize its systems on one computer platform. Most organizations today have heterogeneous computer systems. A company can have an accounting work unit using an IBM mainframe platform while an engineering unit down the hall uses a Hewlett-Packard workstation system. At the warehouse, the inventory system may reside on a Digital Equipment midrange computer. Throughout the organization, individual users work on personal computers. Hardware specialization has its advantages. Network computing allows the system's architect to tie these systems together, providing each work unit a customizable environment while allowing everyone to share documents, drawings, and files from a common electronic filing cabinet.

[Definition]

Local Area Networks (LANs): A network of PCs linked together so that they can communicate and share information. The central hub of the LAN is often called a server.

[Definition]

Wide Area Networks (WANs): Communications vehicles that allow the transmission of voice and video along with normal data transmissions.

Other benefits of network computing are just as persuasive:

- *Cost savings.* The trend we call downsizing (see Chap. 16) applies to networking in spades. The microprocessor has revolutionized every aspect of computing, but none more so than networking. The result is an inexorable trend to more PC-based computing connected by local area networks (LANS), wide area networks (WANs), and other forms of client/server or distributed computing.

- *Scalability.* This is the ability to increment the size and capability of systems to suit specific applications. With host networks, it was often very expensive to allow relatively minor additions to the system. If a host-based system supported a maximum of 48 users and the company had a need to add one user, the cost of networking modifications could well double. The next increment might be a 96-user system. The scalability just wasn't there. Network computing eliminates this problem because the costs of adding a user equal the incremental costs of the hardware and software.

- *Flexibility.* Network computing developed at the same time that corporations all over the world were merged, acquired, and reorganized. Host networks had a very hard time keeping up with all these changes. Network computing can be retargeted much more easily to mirror the information management needs of new organizations. This is so because network computing is more modular, allowing system architects to quickly adjust the placement and relationships of the different supporting computer platforms, using the network as a point of integration.

[Conversation]

A Brief History of Networking

Increased connectivity is a fundamental goal of human beings. Every human initiative, starting with the development of language itself, has been spurred by the need of people to reduce the distance between each other. This is no less true of information technology. The information age, or third wave in Alvin Toffler's terminology, rivals the two other fundamental turning points in human evolution—the agricultural and industrial revolutions—for its impact on every element of human activity.

The development of large networks managed by a centralized mainframe computer perfectly mirrored the society of the 1950s. Using a central computer to manage the communication needs of thousands of users across vast distances, traditional host-based computing made possible large multinational corporations. It helped create the modern switched telephone system and enabled human beings to walk on the moon.

But times changed, and the world needed a newer, more flexible way to communicate and share information. The large, slow moving hierarchical bureaucracies that were so well served by traditional computing yielded to smaller, flattened organizations. These fast moving, streamlined companies demanded more services and the power to chart their own destinies. The master/slave relationship of traditional computing, in which a small group of central administrators charted the course of thousands of voice-less users, obstructed the operational alignment of emerging companies. End users simply rebelled. With or without the cooperation of the centralized data center, they built their own networks. A new system based on peer-to-peer computing appeared.

Networking makes possible a new range of communications poised to change our lives forever. I am referring to technologies such as electronic mail, telecommuting, radio frequency, and interactive television. All the attention being paid to the so-called information superhighway is part of the evolution of networks. The delivery mechanism of the information highway will be glass fiber. It will deliver an abundance of services to offices and houses—entertainment, games, video phone, voting services, and helpful data in many guises. It promises to change the way people work and play.

The highways being constructed today are different from the electronic superhighway that Vice President Al Gore is promoting. His is a national network of supercomputers, linked by fiber optics, that will connect universities, hospitals, research centers, and other institutions that need to exchange vast amounts of data. Construction of this superhighway, an expansion of today's federally subsidized scientific networks, seems almost certain to proceed. But the Clinton administration is counting on private enterprise to construct advanced networks that will serve the general public. As a result, America's information system won't have a single owner: It will be a network of networks, controlled by many companies promoting incompatible systems. A single standard will eventually emerge, but not before leaving a trail of roadkill on the information highway.

19
Application Development

When people talk about the challenge of information technology, what they often think about is programming. Application development has traditionally been one of the weakest links in the software development process, which also includes design, testing, and maintenance. Programming is perceived to be an arcane art practiced by unruly people using mysterious languages. Since the beginning of the industry, organizations have been searching for a way to make all those programmers unnecessary.

[Quotation]

If people built houses the way organizations build strategic information management systems, the first woodpecker that came along would destroy civilization.   ANONYMOUS

Over the years we have seen a number of silver bullet solutions that have promised "programming without programmers." COBOL, the most widely used programming language today, was actually designed to put computer programming into the hands of businesspeople and eliminate the need for programmers. It never happened. While COBOL is much easier to use than the lower-level languages it replaced, it is by no means friendly enough for nontechnical people.

[Definition]

COBOL: Acronym for Common Business-Oriented Language. Programming language designed for business data processing in 1959 by Grace Hopper, a U.S. Navy officer. COBOL programs tend to be wordy, but easy to read, which makes it easier for programmers, other than the original authors, to make corrections or changes. Its original objective, never met, was to eliminate the need for programmers.

Nor are any of the subsequent silver bullets that came along: structured programming, fourth generation languages, CASE, object-oriented programming. All these technologies or methodologies have offered incremental benefits but none of them have threatened the livelihoods of programmers. The hard truth is that, as long as there are programs, there will have to be programmers. In fact, there are still far more COBOL programmers today than any other languages, and I suspect it will be decades before they are replaced. That said, let's take a closer look at two of the more celebrated approaches to improving the application development life cycle.

Computer-Assisted Software Engineering (CASE)

Most computer applications are still crafted by techniques and assumptions that Henry Ford would not find startling. And, like Henry's Model Ts, which were available in any color as long as you wanted black, too many of today's computer systems are rigid, restrictive, and only accidentally of utility to the people who ordered them.

If there was a museum for dead information technologies, computer-assisted software engineering (CASE) would have a wing devoted to it. No other technology in recent memory has been more discredited. Most vendors of CASE technology have quietly dropped the term. Even the premier magazine devoted to the technology changed its name from *CASE Trends* to *Application Development Trends*.

It's important to know about CASE not only as an object lesson—as to what happens when a technology is shamelessly hyped—but because the principles of engineering rigor and discipline underlying it are still sound.

While the objectives of CASE were noble, its goal of imposing engineering rigor on programmers was doomed from the start. Despite the industry's best efforts to make programming respond to a cookie cutter approach, the reality, supported by over 40 years of experience, is that good programming is an art. CASE failed because it attempted the impossible.

But CASE would have failed for two reasons even if it could accomplish the things it was designed to accomplish. The merits of CASE aside, the first reason it failed was that the initiative was imposed by senior management in an unthinking top-down fashion. Line workers resisted CASE because it was jammed down their throats without adequate consultation, preparation, or training.

Hype was the second reason CASE failed. CASE was shamelessly oversold by the vendors, creating an environment of such gross overexpectations that even occasional CASE successes were deemed failures. Based on advertiser claims and widely hyped research studies, customers had wildly distorted expectations of costs (too low), time tables (too optimistic), and results (too high). When reality set in, the backlash was predictable.

The theory of CASE was, and is, sound: The evolution of the application development process has brought organizations to a new level of industrialization. We must learn to build software as we have learned to build appliances. CASE techniques force information technology to restructure itself around a new streamlined application development process to attack enterprise-level information needs.

CASE promised to discipline the system development process. CASE, the theory held, supported users involved in every aspect of the software development life cycle. A CASE approach to software development means that software needs, analysis, design, development, and implementation are coordinated using a computer-based life cycle framework. The major benefit of this approach is that it imposes a discipline on an often undisciplined process. The discipline takes the form of strict project management controls, higher reuse of components, and controlled rather than ad hoc decision making.

Many of the failures of which CASE is accused can be traced to cultural and organizational difficulties. Implementing a CASE methodology makes considerable demands on virtually every aspect of an organization. Few companies have prepared themselves for the required cultural and organizational changes without which CASE implementations cannot be successful. As a consequence, many companies have taken the easy way out and blamed the tools. The fault, however, is not generally with the tools but lack of planning and unreasonable expectations.

Object-Oriented Programming

The revolutionaries would have you believe that object-oriented programming—a genuinely exciting technology—is brand new and should be embraced immediately. The truth is that object-oriented programming was introduced in the 1960s. The real problem is that until very recently, it was of interest mainly to academics because the technology was so difficult to use.

That situation is changing now, as powerful microprocessors with graphical user interfaces make object-oriented programming more intuitive and practical. Still, the technology will have only marginal application until it is cost-effective to migrate existing systems to object-oriented methods. The technology will really take off when its main benefit—the reuse of existing software—can be applied to the millions of existing business applications that need updating.

The principles of object-orientation are not difficult to understand. Object-oriented programming, like a Lego structure, encourages the reuse of chunks (objects) of data, dramatically reducing the time required to develop applications by decreasing the amount of code a developer has to create and maintain. Instead of writing software from scratch, the programmer merely assembles self-contained modules of standardized, prewritten code. To revise a program, the programmer can simply plug in a new module without rewriting the whole thing—a process that helps companies cash in on emerging opportunities by quickly deploying software applications.

We are all inherently familiar with objects because the only way we can accomplish a task is to take action on an object. Our lives are filled with such actions: We start the car, we turn on a PC, we dial a phone, we fax a document, we open a can of Coke. Object-oriented software does the same thing except that the tasks which act on the objects are the traditional functions that programmers used to spend weeks coding.

An object is just a chunk of active data. Unlike passive chunks of data, which just lie there letting procedures manipulate them, an object might be an order or insurance claim complete with text, audio, and video. The order object might know how to process itself through inventory, ship itself, or post itself to accounts receivable. The insurance claim object might evaluate itself. Objects are intelligent in that they contain logic as well as data.

The benefits seem so appealing that now object-orientation is buried in hype and everyone is talking about it. You hear so much about it that you begin to think that it can do everything including cure cancer, repair the ozone layer, and balance the U.S. budget.

In fact, object-oriented technology has a more modest but still highly desirable goal: to generate better software. Object-orientation simplifies the process of programming software by promoting more consistent, smaller, and more error-free applications.

20
Groupware

Everyone is talking about reengineering business through small teams working together in a flattened organization. Groupware, an exciting development in software, actually does something about it.

As a software category, groupware supports the activities of existing workgroups or teams. Groupware creates electronic databases, conferences, and forums that are "open" 24 hours a day, so that people can drop in on meetings at their leisure. Computer Associates, for example, has established a CEO forum on CompuServe for alumni of the CEO Technology Retreats (discussed in Chap. 12).

The current interest in groupware is being driven by the pursuit of enhanced workgroup effectiveness. This is a dramatic shift from the first 10 years of personal computing, when most software developers targeted personal productivity. While most PC software has been designed for people working alone, these programs make it easier for groups to work and learn together.

The bottom line is aligned with the use of groupware in that companies are trying to do more work faster with fewer people. Time compression means less time for making decisions and that small groups rather than individuals or large committees will be the agents getting things done.

On one level, groupware is fairly obvious: It consists simply of tools that support collaborative work and the sharing of information in the pursuit of workgroup goals and objectives. For example, a team using groupware can create a document, complete with an audit trail of the contributions of each team member.

Groupware adds a new dimension to electronic mail. While E-mail works fine for sending a message to an individual or group—communicating one-to-one or one-to-many—groupware allows a new, more powerful variety of communication: many-to-many. It's not uncommon, for instance, for someone to send an electronic memo to everyone in the department. Groupware enables the kind of many-to-many interactions that have been seen to deliver enormous productivity gains for corporations.

Groupware has a profound implication on an organization's culture. If information is power, groupware redefines the way power is distributed in an organization. In this way, groupware virtually compels companies to reengineer themselves. The good news: By making previously restricted information available to workers throughout the organization, groupware empowers people closest to the customers. The bad news: Groupware is devastating to managers who act as gatekeepers for information flowing from the field to the apex of the organization or vice versa.

[Definition]

Electronic Mail (E-mail): Generic term for computer applications that enable users to send messages to other users at different computers. More than any other technology since the invention of the telephone, electronic mail has changed the way businesspeople communicate.

Indiscriminate use of groupware has been associated with information overload. When messages are promiscuously dispatched to everyone, managers have to be orderly about what information they seek out. Fortunately, most groupware allows individuals to filter incoming information in elegant and creative ways. Other users impose brute force limits on groupware. I know one executive who, out of desperation, now refuses groupware messages from anyone not directly reporting to him.

Groupware is highly addictive, so you must be vigilant against groupware junkies. Electronic mail is important but it must not displace other vital activities of the organization such as face-to-face communications with colleagues, meetings with customers, and meeting project commitments. At CA , we have evolved strict policies on the use of our worldwide E-mail network. For example, CA employees are, by policy, restricted from using the E-mail system during the key business hours of 10:00 A.M. to noon and 2:00–4:00 P.M., local time. The system has been designed to reject E-mail during these periods. CA users working on the E-mail system at 9:59 A.M. and 1:59 p.m. will get a message warning them to save their work. We have found that this policy promotes judicious use of the E-mail network.

21

Business Issues

The most critical issue in managing information technology is management. The truth is that business issues always supersede technology issues, although the disconnected organization too often reverses that reality. Consider issues such as outsourcing, business process reengineering, and quality. While they heavily impact information technology, questions of reengineering, quality, and outsourcing are fundamentally business issues. They are best considered in that light.

Outsourcing

Outsourcing, in its current meaning of handing over management of an organization's information technology resource to an outside service company, entered the vocabulary of CEOs in July, 1989. In that month, Eastman Kodak Co. announced that it was stripping away its computer operations, lock, stock, and mainframe, and farming them out.

The news shocked corporate America. Granted, outsourcing had been around for years—most corporations had long outsourced their payroll application—but it was usually a quick fix or to save money by offloading routine information technology needs that offered no real strategic value. Now here was a household name—Number 18 on the Fortune 500—infusing the term with a whole new meaning. Kodak outsourced its considerable information technology resource as a major strategic move designed not only to reduce expenses but to improve competitiveness and serve key business goals.

We can debate whether the strategy was sound. But certainly there can be no argument that in the next five years the outsourcing bandwagon gained considerable momentum. It's hard to pick up the business pages of the newspaper without reading about yet another company that has signed an outsourcing agreement.

Only a few years ago, outsourcing was a niche activity that organizations used as a short-term solution or to offload non-value-added activities. Companies tended to apply outsourcing as a temporary, functional fix while management attended to some larger problem. Today's take on outsourcing is entirely different—thanks, in large part, to a whole new business environment.

In its new meaning, outsourcing refers to an organization that hires an outside contractor to handle all or part of its information technology functions. Outsourcing arrangements, today, tend to be long-term rather than short-term and strategic rather than functional. In some cases, the contractor acquires the organization's hardware and assumes responsibility for the existing information technology staff. In other cases, the contractor uses its own equipment and staff. Whatever the arrangement, the contractor is responsible for managing the day-to-day operations and meeting defined objectives. The company, in turn, pays the outsourcer on a contract-service basis.

Outsourcing appeals to many CEOs and financial executives because they understand it. CEOs can take information technology, which is something they struggle with and which is costing them more and more money each year, and replace it with a fixed-cost contract, a concept they understand very well. Outsourcing typically shifts numbers from the capital budget to the operating budget. This they understand very well, too.

Outsourcing and the disconnect are linked to the extent that outsourcing promises a shortcut around the very real challenges of understanding and managing information technology. But the central message in this book is that there is no substitute for understanding and managing information technology. As with all shortcuts that take you over unexplored territory, it is easy to lose your way.

[Definition]

Outsourcing: The transfer of assets—computers, networks, and people— from within an organization to an outside service vendor that takes responsibility for the outsourced activity.

Not all outsourcing is undesirable. Selective outsourcing makes sense in selected situations. It can sometimes reduce operating costs because of the economies of scale an outsourcer can bring to bear. An outsourcing company can justify a much more efficient but more costly computer than could an individual company because it can spread that cost around to dozens of subscribers. Theoretically, it can then pass along the savings to the individual companies.

Outsourcing can also meet needs that are difficult to satisfy in-house. Payroll is still an excellent candidate for outsourcing. Payroll regulations across jurisdictions change so quickly that it makes good sense for large multi-site companies to entrust this application to a specialist. Specialized applications such as fulfillment and delivery are other functions that might be cost-effectively handled by an outsourcer.

Having an outsourcer provide an outsourcing proposal can serve as an excellent way to benchmark an information technology function. If the outsourcer is prepared to manage the function for less than current costs, management definitely needs to understand why. If the outsourcer can manage the function for less and still make a profit, the outsourcing proposal should give some good clues as to where the inefficiencies are. While the organization can certainly elect to save money by signing the proposal, it can also use the proposal as a wakeup call to its information technology people.

Selective outsourcing can also help a company concentrate on its strategic mission. It can help a company quickly enter an information technology-intensive business. For companies that are seriously handicapped in hardware or human resources, selective outsourcing can represent significant dollar and time savings. With hardware life cycles growing shorter, making it difficult for companies to achieve payback, it becomes a real challenge to plan for technology upgrades. Selective outsourcing offloads this problem very neatly. For situations like these, outsourcing should be considered as one of many options.

What we don't understand are the long-term implications of general outsourcing. My view is that information technology has become an indispensable means of seizing competitive advantage. In a functional way, outsourcing turns over control of that expertise to what is really another company. How wise is it, really, to entrust your information assets to outside hands? This is the information you depend on to retain your customers and suppliers. This is the information that defines your organization. I have to believe that organizations that outsource too much of their information technology expertise will suffer in the long run. At some point in the evolution of an organization that has outsourced its information technology function, the board of directors may determine it is competitively advantageous to reconstitute a dedicated information technology function. But I believe it will be difficult or impossible for many organizations to rebuild a world-class information technology function after relying on service providers for many years.

When companies decide to outsource their data centers, they almost always offer the same justifications. I remain skeptical of many of them. Here are some of the most common justifications and my thoughts.

Outsourcing will lower our information costs. You may be able to achieve the same savings on your own. While costs may, indeed, go down if your information technology resource is run in a sloppy manner, the answer is to clean up the mess, not hand it off to someone else. The much ballyhooed outsourcing cost reductions of a few years ago came as the most inefficient operations were taken over. I saw some of those operations and, let me tell you, things were so bad that a team of hamsters could have saved money. But for reasonably well run information technology shops, the savings may not be there past the first couple of years.

Outsourcing our information systems will allow us to concentrate on our core business. Your core business is information. I don't care if your operation makes doorknobs or services fire alarms, your core business is information.

Outsourcing will reduce our recruiting and training headaches. Recruiting and training represent strategic opportunities to build the talent that will deliver the competitive edge for tomorrow. It's a responsibility the organization cannot delegate and still remain in control of its destiny.

Outsourcing will eliminate the uncertainty that comes with shorter system life cycles. Outsourcing doesn't eliminate the uncertainty, it merely shifts the risk to an entity that may be more interested in protecting its own interests than yours. Besides, the risk of shorter hardware life cycles is often offset by the fact that the cost of the hardware is also falling.

I'm not alone in my skepticism with regard to outsourcing. Dr. Michael Hammer worries that outsourcing may complicate the jobs of CEOs. "Companies run the risk [by outsourcing] of throwing out the baby with the bath water, the baby being the capacity for transformation, the bath water being commodity-like information technology activities," Hammer argues. "In their rush to outsource, I'm afraid that some organizations are outsourcing not just routines that can be handled on a third party basis, but also their body of technical insight. Consequently, when they try to transform themselves, they will lack the skills and capabilities in their organizations that they will need."

The best alternative to outsourcing is sometimes insourcing. Look within. Insourcing is the term used to denote an organization restructuring its information technology operations but retaining full control. Companies can find the talent they need from within their own ranks. While you may need outsiders to help you uncover or develop those talents, you don't have to start from scratch. By insourcing, an organization with computing resources dispersed over a number of data centers may be able to generate the same economies of scale that outsourcers claim for themselves. Like outsourcing companies, insourcers can: consolidate data centers, aggressively negotiate hardware prices, and automate operations to reduce staff and improve service levels.

You can't subcontract your soul. What makes Federal Express Federal Express? What makes United Airlines United Airlines? Every company has a unique something that cannot be outsourced.

[Exercise]

Should You Outsource Your Data Center?

1. Do you experience data center staff turnover of more than 10 percent per year?
   [ ] Yes   [ ] No

2. Are you projecting data center personnel costs, including recruitment, to rise by more than 5 percent per year?
   [ ] Yes   [ ] No

3. Are total data center expenses growing faster than corporate revenue?
   [ ] Yes   [ ] No

4. Is the data center able to recover all data center expenses from end users without complaints?
   [ ] Yes   [ ] No

5. Is more than half of the data center applications portfolio over five years old?
   [ ] Yes   [ ] No

6. Is your CPU routinely operating at over 75 percent capacity?
   [ ] Yes   [ ] No

7. Are you anticipating starting a major information systems project (requiring over 25 percent of data center resources) in the next year?
   [ ] Yes   [ ] No

8. Does your company have a tradition of using consultants, systems integrators, and other service providers?
   [ ] Yes   [ ] No

9. Would it be difficult for your chief executive officer to articulate your company's information systems strategy?
   [ ] Yes   [ ] No

10. Could the capital designated to upgrade the data center be more strategically used for other aspects of the business?
    [ ] Yes   [ ] No

Scoring: Score one point for each Yes answer.

10 points:	Run, don't walk, for immediate help. If you don't want to fix it yourself, outsourcing will save you money.
8-9 points:	We don't have to tell you that your data center is definitely experiencing problems. Consider outsourcing to see what a reasonable approach would cost. Use the outsourcer's proposal as a benchmark. Adjust as necessary.
6-7 points:	You have an average operation. You may or may not see immediate cost benefits from selective outsourcing, but it would be worth a look just to compare.
4-5 points:	Your data center operates better than most. Outsourcing probably cannot cut costs or boost service levels.

0-3 points: Outsourcing can't do a thing for you. You can, however, teach a thing or two to outsourcing providers.

Business Process Reengineering

Business process reengineering (BPR)—one of today's hottest buzzwords—is actually a misnomer. *Reengineering* implies that business processes were "engineered" in the first place. This has rarely been the case.

BPR is such a hot topic today precisely because the cumulative effects of 50 years of static business assumptions and processes are now intolerable. So in the best tradition of the disconnect, the gurus of BPR propose a massive, radical transformation that typically involves throwing out existing investments in favor of something new. Sound familiar? While there is much in business to transform and however compelling the promises of reengineering may be, it seems to me that BPR is a poor substitute for continual zero-based thinking.

BPR is not necessary for organizations that periodically reinvent themselves. Such companies examine every procedure, every process, every policy in light of a few simple questions:

- Does it make sense?
- Why are we doing this?
- Why should our customers care if we do it at all?
- Would we be better off doing something else?

When a CEO insists that these tough questions be asked and that appropriate steps be taken based on the answers, *that* is true business process reengineering. Unfortunately, most organizations are victims of their own success. The most difficult thing in the world is to question the practices that made you rich. Yet that is precisely what every CEO must do. Most companies are trapped by inertia until changing conditions so threaten their survival that company managers begin to think that even the perils of BPR are preferable to doing nothing.

Most companies today can trace their work styles back to the 1700s, when Adam Smith articulated the principle of division of labor. Smith observed that some number of specialized workers, each performing a single step in the manufacture of a pin, could make far more pins in a day than the same number of generalists, each engaged in making whole pins.

Today's companies have all been built around Smith's central idea—the division of labor and the consequent fragmentation of work. The larger the organization, the more specialized is the work and the more separate the steps into which the work is fragmented.

The information age imposes new realities on organizations. The old ways of doing business—assuming a constant, predictable environment—simply don't work anymore. In today's environment, nothing is constant or predictable. The overall process of producing or delivering a good or service inevitably has become increasingly complicated. Managing such processes tests the best teams of decision makers who must work with antiquated processes.

In reengineering, business people must focus on processes, not functions. Don't think in terms of departments; think in terms of business outcomes. For example, the order management process may involve numerous functional activities such as sales, customer service, credit, and fulfillment, but it must be viewed as an integrated process. Similarly, the fulfillment process spans logistics, manufacturing, and finance activities.

Business process reengineering generally begins with a blank slate approach. One must operate outside the constraints of traditional thinking and not be bound by historical precedent. As such, the goal is quantum, not incremental, improvement. For example, one company has adapted a "10 ×" goal; employees are striving to improve operational efficiency tenfold.

Reengineering involves, but is not limited to, changes to a company's information technology infrastructure. Information technology enhancements are often an important consideration, but are meaningless without substantial simplification of the business processes.

Reengineering tries to focus accountability and responsibility. Most activities should be performed within a focused cell, where an individual or group can have responsibility for the entire task. This change empowers employees in new ways and enriches their jobs, as well as allowing for markedly higher efficiencies. It also concentrates on eliminating waste and improving the speed of operational and administrative activities. It forces a company to continually question what value is added in every task performed. If no value is added, the task is eliminated.

Finally, it is useful to consider what reengineering is not. It is not the same as reorganizing, delayering, or flattening the organization, although reengineering may produce a flatter organization. The problems facing companies result not from their organizational structures but from their process structures. Overlaying a new organization on top of an old process is like rearranging the deck chairs on the Titanic.

"Fundamentally, true business reengineering is about reversing the Industrial Revolution," write Michael Hammer and James Champy in *Reengineering the Corporation:*

> Reengineering rejects the assumptions inherent in Adam Smith's industrial paradigm—the division of labor, economies of scale, hierarchical control, and all the other appurtenances of an early-stage developing economy, and it forces managers to search for new models for organizing work. Tradition counts for nothing. Reengineering is a new beginning.

CEOs have bought into the reengineering concept in a big way. CIOs, by and large, have not. Surveys suggest that sharp differences between CEOs and CIOs are developing over reengineering and other high-profile technology topics. For example, a survey conducted by Gateway Management Consulting in New

York shows that 88 percent of CEOs list business process engineering as their improvement program of choice, yet only 2 percent of CIOs agree. And while 77 percent of CEOs are fired up over restructuring, another form of reengineering, none of the CIOs surveyed showed similar enthusiasm for the concept.

The disconnect neatly accounts for the discrepancy in the level of excitement demonstrated by CEOs and CIOs. Initiatives such as reengineering are typically top-down decisions, formulated by corporate managers and imposed on departmental workgroups such as Accounting, Engineering, and Information Technology. Rarely do the workgroups participate in the planning for such processes. Rather, they are expected to comply without having ownership in the activities. People who feel disenfranchised by the disconnect naturally resist.

[Definition]

Business Process Reengineering: The fundamental rethinking and radical redesign of business processes to achieve dramatic improvements in critical contemporary measures of performance such as cost, quality, service, and speed. (From *Reengineering the Corporation* by Michael Hammer and James Champy.)

[Conversation]

Ten Principles of Business Process Reengineering

1. Before you ask how (How are we going to do this?), ask what if? (What if we don't do this at all?)

2. Really understand the purpose of the process; don't just describe it.

3. Organize around business outcomes, not tasks.

4. Have those who use the output of the process perform the process (if you need pencils, you order the pencils).

5. Subsume information technology work into the real work that produces the information.

6. Think cross-functionally.

7. Treat geographically dispersed resources as though they were centralized.

8. Link parallel activities instead of integrating their results.

9. Put the decision point where the work is performed and build control into the process: Make employees responsible.

10. Capture information once and at the source; avoid redundant storage of information.

SOURCE: *Reinventing the Corporation*, Michael Hammer and James Champy.

Quality

How has the concept of quality changed in the years you've been in business? Profoundly. Customers expect quality systems today and settle for nothing less.

It wasn't always so. For example, in years past, customers expected a certain level of defects; downtime and an acceptable level of bugs was viewed as the norm. No longer. Customers have become less tolerant of poor quality, whether it be in terms of manufacturing defects in General Motors automobiles or errors in Hertz rent-a-car reservations. It is axiomatic in this day and age that organizations without a quality program in place enjoy a prominent spot on the endangered species list.

Quality is rapidly becoming the principle focus of senior managers in every environment. The quality emphasis is less on doing things right than on doing the right things. There is always the danger of doing the wrong things exceedingly well. A good set of quality metrics looks at customer satisfaction as the most reliable measurement for any enterprise.

One of the most important requirements of any quality initiative is a total focus on the customer or client. While other quality control theories seek out problems, assign fault, and attempt to effect improvement by exhorting people to change their behavior, quality programs seek to understand processes and revise them using data about the processes themselves.

Another essential feature of quality programs is the concept of continuously seeking improvement in quality by eliminating all activities that do not add value to the process of providing quality. Non-value activities are considered "waste" and are candidates for elimination.

The conventional wisdom is that poor quality is invariably expensive while high quality may actually reduce costs. Improvements in quality can improve revenues or reduce costs, both of which improve the bottom line. As client needs are better satisfied, revenues usually increase. For example, new services or revisions of existing services to better meet specific client needs often generate more revenue. The challenge is to reorient employees so they think about the high cost of non-value added activities, such as those that do not affect the bottom line.

[Conversation]

Computer Associates Quality Commitment

Just as every organization benefits from formulating a mission statement, I think that organizations should also draft a quality commitment. It's not a trivial process to articulate a quality commitment, but it's well worth the effort. On the reverse of the business cards of every one of CA's 7000 employees around the world is the following quality commitment:

- To provide defect-free products and services in partnership with our clients and each other.

- To fully define and understand the requirements of our jobs and the systems that support us in meeting the changing needs of our clients.

- To conform to those requirements—on time, every time.

Part 4
Connect

As a young programmer working at Columbia University, I heard a story that may be to the point here. Dwight Eisenhower, before he became President of the United States, served as president of Columbia, a university which, like all Ivy League colleges, took pride in the well manicured lawns of its campus.

One day, Eisenhower received a frantic appeal from the head groundskeeper. The students, ignoring multiple warnings to please stay off the grass, were wearing unsightly paths through the lush grass of the main quadrangle. Would the president use his authority to make the students stop trespassing on the lawn?

"Why do they walk on the grass?" Eisenhower asked.

"Because it is the quickest way to get from the main entrance to the central hall," the groundskeeper said.

"If that's the way the students are going to go," he said, "then put a pathway there." Problem solved.

Every army general in history learns one thing about leadership: A leader is the one who notices which way the troops march and then gets out in front. Eisenhower knew it is folly to resist people validating the fundamental principle that the shortest distance between two points is a straight line.

All this is by way of saying that, when fundamental things are happening, it is ultimately futile to stand in the way. If you're not part of the steamroller, you're part of the road. It is so much better to recognize the inevitable and make it work for you. You don't need to know all the details to adjust your life to the facts. Flexibility in accepting change is just as important as flexibility in resisting it. The important thing is not to ignore the thousands of signs all around you that point like flashing neon lights to the fact that it can't be business as usual anymore. One of the clearest markers are pathways worn by thousands of feet in what was thought to be no-man's land.

The evolution of the connected organization is another of those fundamental forces in the affairs of men and women. The changing shape of this new organizational structure can and should be channeled, but the reality that it is changing cannot be blocked or argued away. In this book, I have tried to suggest some ways in which the new partnership between CEOs and CIOs can be channeled. I have also tried to argue that resistance to this new model is not only counterproductive, it is futile. In this last section, I offer some landmarks that will help readers recognize the as-yet little worn paths to the connected organization. I also suggest there is no reason why the earliest feet to explore those paths should not be yours.

[Quotation]

You said "but." I've put my finger on the whole trouble. You're a "but" man. Don't say "but." That little word "but" is the difference between success and failure.

Henry Ford said, "I'm going to invent the automobile," and Arthur T. Flanken said, "But ..."

SGT. ERNIE BILKO
"The Phil Silvers Show"

22

If You Want Things to Change, You Have to Change Things

Let's agree, then, to eliminate the gulf that has existed between CEOs and CIOs and between their respective staffs. As a CEO, I believe the job must start at the CEO level. As a technologist, I'm certain of it. While the work of eliminating the disconnect involves every corner of the organization and must engage the talents and resolve of every participant, the task must begin with the chief executive. The CEO must be the main advocate of any meaningful transformation. The buck not only stops here, it starts with the CEO.

I am confident that the attitude of the CEO will be the most significant determinant in organizations making the transition to the connected organization. Let me close *Techno Vision* with a few observations about what those attitudes will entail:

Articulate a vision that is germane to the business.
Without a bold vision of business, clearly articulated and effectively implemented, well aligned information technology is irrelevant. However, the technology is the necessary base and
business enabler. If that base is not conspicuously in place or
does not work reliably, there is little if anything to enable. The
vision must have hooks at every level. It must be broad enough
to inspire buy-in from everyone in the organization, leaving no
one out, yet specific enough to inspire information technology
initiatives at the grass roots level.

There is a fine line between vision and hallucination.
Steve Jobs, originally of Apple and now of NeXT, has a forceful,
visionary outlook that changed the face of the computer industry and perhaps the world. His was a vision that was well
defended against inconvenient facts. He pressed everyone, especially doubters, to align with his vision. Sometimes Jobs'
persistence paid off. More often, it failed. While his place in
history is assured, it's not as a CEO. Jobs' leadership didn't allow
for collaboration; his colleagues eventually suspended their
own judgment when they entered what was termed Jobs' reality
distortion field.

My point is that CEOs of the connected organization need all
the help they can get. Teamwork cannot be sustained in an
environment that shouts down naysayers. If your vision cannot
survive attack, it may not be worth defending. There can be no
assistance from colleagues whose best judgment is suspended
in deference to your vision.

[Interview]

Technology Vision?
Frankly, My Dear, I Don't Give a Damn.

*Charles, who is responsible for articulating the technology vision
of a company? The CIO or the CEO?*

Who gives a damn about the technology vision? Does the CEO of Wal-Mart care about the technology vision? He cares about whether Wal-Mart's distribution system can get product to the stores just before the customer walks in. He cares about whether Wal-Mart's inventory system has integrated suppliers so intimately that replenishment stock is on its way within minutes after the customer walks out of the store. If it doesn't help the customer, it's not germane to the conversation. Technology vision is not germane to the customer.

Doesn't someone have to have the big picture?

Yes, but what does that have to do with technology vision? Maybe the way to create value is to start with a strong vision, but then ruthlessly abandon parts of that vision to uncover some greater truth.

Truths like what?

Truths like that we spend too much time formulating visionary strategies that have little or nothing to do with the customer. Most technology vision looks inward, not outward. The CEO and the CIO must be concerned with meeting the needs of customers, developing new products and services, and thinking ahead. This has surprisingly little to do with the technology vision, which in any case doesn't exist. There is never *the* technology vision; there are always as many technology visions as there are challenges. And the targets are constantly shifting.

How do you know when the information technology and business goals are well aligned?

When all the information technology systems look deceptively simple. The more complex the systems are, the less likely the technology is focused on anything important. Every system should be focused on the customer. If an initiative doesn't make sense for the customer, it shouldn't get done. It's that simple.

At some point, shouldn't the CEO expect the CIO to propose the proper focus of information technology at the company?

Absolutely not. It's got to be the CEO's technology focus. And that means the CEO needs to know the technology issues. In this context, CEOs need to be their own chief information officers. They have to be thoroughly engaged in the process; CIOs can only be their guides and helpers.

An ounce of application is worth a ton of abstraction.   I
have a bias for action. Do something and see if it works. I admire
one company with a creative program for getting executives and
computers together. This company invites the teenage sons and
daughters of executives to come into the office on weekends
where they are trained on the various office information systems. At that point, the company sends the systems home with
the teenagers so that the kids can train the executives in the
comfort of their homes. The systems are already loaded with
relevant corporate data. As the executives learn the system, they
work with real corporate data so that they can immediately see
the value of analyzing data.

There is no such thing as a technology-neutral decision.
The information technology element of business is becoming
dominant and transparent. Information technology per se can
no longer be divorced from the myriad decisions CEOs have to
make. Organizations are pure information processing machines.
Their job is to capture, massage, and channel information. The
information processing infrastructure you enable (for it won't
be enabled otherwise) will increasingly differentiate your company from the competition. Only information technology will
create the connections between your product or service and the
customer. Because every decision you make has an information
technology implication, it is vital for you to be informed and
comfortable with the strategic issues. The quality and quantity
of information comprehended per unit of time may now determine who wins or loses, whether the issue is a customer order
or a national war.

**Information technology doesn't support the business; it
is the business.**   I cannot be clearer than this: Give up any
idea you may have about how information technology can
support your business. Your business is information and information is your business.

Information technology changes everything you have ever
learned about business management. It has changed the very
meaning of management and the skills needed to do it well.

Information technology flattens management. It has already flattened millions of managers who have failed to accommodate themselves to the inevitable. Forces like this make no exceptions. Even for you—maybe especially for you.

Please don't feel that you're being singled out. You're in good company. Everyone—your colleagues, your competitors, even your customers—is reeling. Thanks to the transformation inspired by information technology, every economic activity is up for renegotiation.

So deeply embedded in every process that it is all but invisible, information technology will underlie every business activity in the connected organization. Information technology will not be considered a tool or even a way to leverage human knowledge. It will become an expected utility, much like electricity, noticeable only in the rare event it is withdrawn.

New roles for the CIO. Look for a new model of the CIO's role in the connected organization. The new CIO will be more focused on the enterprise infrastructure (in fact, *CIO* may well be redefined as chief infrastructure officer). The primary job of the CIO will be to guard and control the process of acquiring knowledge. The CIO will help learning organizations remain flexible by designing highly adaptive information processes and systems. As ambassadors working closely with the business units, CIOs will help rethink and transform operations through information technology.

CEO as chief nudger. If you never hear the CIO say "No!" during the realignment, you're not pushing hard enough. To the extent the organization has a technology vision, it must be the CEO's vision. Moreover, the vision should be outrageous. I believe it's deadly for a CEO to articulate a vision that turns out to be too low. People or organizations rarely attain goals higher than those they set for themselves. They look to the CEO for scope. It is the job of the CEO to recalibrate the objectives of the enterprise such that there is no possibility of the organization ever exceeding it.

[Conversation]

Sync or Swim: Seven Steps to Being the Best

1. *Benchmark to determine the world standard.* Some organization has to be the best. Why not yours? Find the world champion in every process—technical and otherwise—that you measure. Do the benchmarks to determine how your performance compares. Recalibrate your goals accordingly.

2. *Map your processes.* Break down activities into processes. Identify the inefficiencies. Reinvent. For each step, ask whether customers, if given a choice, would pay for it.

3. *Get your people focused on external reality.* The issue is customers and competitors. Define a clear vision that creates a sense of urgency. Insist that people accept responsibility for their own behavior.

4. *Start with the hardest part.* Distinguish what needs to be done from how hard it is to do it. The most difficult steps are generally the most important. Model the attitude that if something really needs to be done, the difficulty of doing it is irrelevant.

5. *Set the goals high and then double them.* Your people will rise to the challenge if you support them properly. Set the goal, but don't tell them how to do it. Their ideas will be better than yours. If people fail to reach the goal, don't punish them; adjust your support.

6. *Let go and watch.* You can't do it alone. So kick back and enjoy.

7. *Wave laurels, don't rest on them.* When you're on top of the mountain, it's natural to want to relax. Take a minute and enjoy the view. But hang on. It's windy up there. You won't have privacy for long. Your competitors—benchmarks in hand—are within hailing distance.

[Joke]

You Want to be CEO? Jump in the Pool

A CEO throwing a party takes his executives on a tour of his opulent mansion. In the back of the property, the CEO has the largest swimming pool any of them has ever seen. The huge pool, however, is filled with hungry alligators. The CEO says to his executives: "I think an executive should be measured by courage. Courage is what made me CEO. So this is my challenge to each of you: If anyone has enough courage to dive into the pool, swim through those alligators, and make it to the other side, I will give that person anything they desire. My job, my money, my house, anything!"

Everyone laughs at the outrageous offer and proceeds to follow the CEO on the tour of the estate. Suddenly, they hear a loud splash. Everyone looks around and sees the CIO in the pool, swimming for his life. He dodges the alligators left and right and makes it to the edge of the pool with seconds to spare. The CIO pulls himself out just as a huge alligator snaps off the CIO's shoes.

The flabbergasted CEO approaches the CIO and says, "You are amazing. I've never seen anything like it in my life. You are brave beyond measure and anything I own is yours. Tell me what I can do for you."

The CIO, panting for breath, looks up and says, "You can do one thing for me. Tell me, who the hell pushed me in the pool?"

If all objections must first be overcome, nothing would be attempted.   There are, no doubt, many objections against embracing the connected organization. There are certainly many land mines on the road, and I'll take bets that we will encounter every single one of them. More than a few people will defend the status quo. Opposition and protest will fly fast and furiously from those who are scared or threatened, as well as from those who are sincere and occasionally even accurate. The committed CEO will not feel the need to have an answer for every objection. Some changes cannot be completely planned. They have to unfold.

[Quotation]

The deadline for complaints was yesterday.

CHARLES B. WANG
Chairman and CEO, Computer Associates International

In the long term, put first things first. CEOs must combine two attitudes that don't often come easy: taking the long-term point of view and putting first things first. The American economic engine has long been criticized for rewarding short-termism. CEOs must decide to resist that pressure and cultivate the payoffs that come from research and development, quality initiatives, strategic partnerships, and other long-term activities. For many CEOs this will mean evolving a more balanced approach to measuring progress. A balanced scorecard not only reflects traditional values such as financial results and shareholder value, but strategic, technical, sociological, and environmental considerations as well.

[Quotation]

If all else fails, immortality can always be assured by spectacular error.

JOHN KENNETH GALBRAITH
American economist and author, 1908–

Ending the disconnect requires a mind set, not a skill set. In the last analysis, ending the disconnect is a decision that starts with the CEO and is sustained by every participant in the organization. There are no secret formulas, magic potions, or shortcuts. Everything you need to start the transformation is available to you. You have but to decide and act.

Will it be easy? Don't kid yourself. The unavoidable truth is that all change comes at great cost, for the guilty and sometimes for the innocent. The approaching business transformation will not be different. The transformation will require all participants to revise the way in which they now deal with one another and with the outside world. To live in this world, all of us must make changes in our lives.

The lines defining the disconnect don't simply go away. Someone has to erase them. But eliminating the disconnect is not, by itself, a goal worth fighting for. Our efforts will be measured not by what we erase but by what we build.

[Anecdote]

No Problem, I'll Change Course!

A battleship had been at sea in heavy weather for several days. The visibility was poor with patchy fog, so the captain remained on the bridge keeping an eye on all activities.

Shortly after dark, the lookout on the wing of the bridge reported, "Light, bearing on the starboard bow."

"Is it steady or moving astern?" the captain called out.

Lookout replied, "Steady, captain," which meant the battleship was on a dangerous collision course.

The captain then called to the signalman, "Signal that ship: We are on a collision course, advise you change course 20 degrees."

Back came a signal, "Advisable for *you* to change course 20 degrees."

The captain said, "Send, I'm a captain, change course 20 degrees."

"I'm a seaman second class," came the reply. "You had better change course 20 degrees."

By that time, the captain was furious. He spat out, "Send, I'm a battleship. Change course 20 degrees."

Back came the flashing reply, "I'm a lighthouse."

The battleship changed course.

References

Allen, Dean O. 1993. "Twenty Questions for Dean O. Allen." *Enterprise Systems Journal.* Feb. vol. 13. no. 2. p.10.

Atre, Shaku. 1994. From a private conversation.

Bennis, Warren G. 1992. *Quotable Business* by Louis E. Boone. New York: Random House.

Brynjolfsson, Erik and Hitt, Loren. 1994. " The Big Payoff from Computers." *Fortune Magazine.* March 7. vol. 127. no. 7. p. 28.

Burris, Peter. 1993. "One on One." *Midrange Systems.* Oct. 26. vol. 6. no. 20. p. 62.

Chesterfield, Lord. 1990. *Leadership* by William Safire and Leonard Safir. New York: Simon & Schuster.

Clarke, Arthur C. 1977. *Peter's Quotations: Ideas for Our Time* by Dr. Laurence J. Peter. New York: Bantam Books.

Crall, Michael J. 1993. From a private conversation.

Crisp, Quentin. 1994. *Executive's Book of Quotations* by Julia Vitullo-Martin and J. Robert Moskin. New York: Oxford University Press.

Dataquest. 1993. "Downsizing Clearly Had an Impact." *PC Magazine.* March 16. vol. 12. no. 5 p. 32.

Davis, Stan and Davidson, Bill. 1992. *2020 Vision.* New York: Simon & Schuster.

Drucker, Peter. 1994. From the "Introduction" to *Techno Vision* by Charles B. Wang. New York: McGraw-Hill.

Elsesser, James R. 1993. From a private conversation.

Firdman, Henry Eric. 1993. "20 Questions for Eric Firdman." *Enterprise Systems Journal.* April. vol. 13. no. 4. p. 10.

Forrester Research, Inc. 1992. "When to Murder Your Mainframe." *Fortune Magazine.* Nov. vol. 126. no. 23. p. 110.

Galbraith, John Kenneth. 1994. *Executive's Book of Quotations* by Julia Vitullo-Martin and J. Robert Moskin. New York: Oxford University Press.

Gardner, John W. 1994. *Executive's Book of Quotations* by Julia Vitullo-Martin and J. Robert Moskin. New York: Oxford University Press.

George, David Lloyd. 1992. *Quotable Business* by Louis E. Boone. New York: Random House.

Half, Robert. 1992. *Quotable Business* by Louis E. Boone. New York: Random House.

Hammer, Michael. 1992. "One on One with John Kador." *Midrange Systems.* August 4. vol. 5. no. 15. p. 38.

Hammer, Michael, and Champy, James. 1993. *Reengineering the Corporation.* New York: Harper Collins.

Harkness, Warren L. 1993. "CIOs Put the 'T' Back in IT." *Datamation.* Dec 1. vol. 39. no. 23. p. 23.

Hayes, Frederick O.R. 1990. *Leadership* by William Safire and Leonard Safir. New York: Simon & Schuster.

Heinlein, Robert. 1977. *Peter's Quotations: Ideas for Our Time* by Dr. Laurence J. Peter. New York: Bantam Books.

Johnson, Nancy. 1992. *Liberation Management* by Tom Peters. New York: Knopf.

Johnson, Samuel. 1992. *Quotable Business* by Louis E. Boone. New York: Random House.

Kozol, Jonathan. 1990. *Life 101* by John Roger and Peter McWilliams. Los Angeles: Prelude Press.

Long, Earl. 1994. *Executive's Book of Quotations* by Julia Vitullo-Martin and J. Robert Moskin. New York: Oxford University Press.

McMennamy, Roger N. 1993. From a private conversation.

Merlyn, Vaughn. 1998. From a private conversation.

National Research Council. 1994. *Information Technology in the Service Society.* Washington, D.C.: National Academy Press.

Peters, Tom. 1992. *Liberation Management* by Tom Peters. New York: Knopf.

Peterson, Robert B. 1993. From a private conversation.

Quadracci, Harry. 1992. *Quotable Business* by Louis E. Boone. New York: Random House.

Rubin, Howard. 1994. From a private conversation.

Schussel, George. 1992. From a private conversation.

Senge, Peter. 1990. *The Fifth Discipline* by Peter Senge. "The Art and Practice of the Learning Organization." New York: Doubleday.

Shaw, George Bernard. 1977. *Peter's Quotations: Ideas for Our Time* by Dr. Laurence J. Peter. New York: Bantam Books.

Sitkin, Irwin J. 1993. "CIOs put the 'T' back in IT." *Datamation.* Dec 1. vol. 39. no. 23. p. 28.

Solow, Robert M. 1991. "IS Spending: Is It out of Control?" *Information Week.* October 14. p. 34.

Steenburgh, Eric. 1993. From a private conversation.

Stimson, Henry. 1977. *Peter's Quotations: Ideas for Our Time* by Dr. Laurence J. Peter. New York: Bantam Books.

Thoreau, Henry David. 1977. *Peter's Quotations: Ideas for Our Time* by Dr. Laurence J. Peter. New York: Bantam Books.

Tinker, Grant. 1994. *Executive's Book of Quotations* by Julia Vitullo-Martin and J. Robert Moskin. New York: Oxford University Press.

Watson, Tom. An often heard anecdote.

Weinshenk, Susan. 1994. From a private conversation.

Wells, George D. 1993. From a private conversation.

Wohl, Amy. 1987. From a private conversation.

Index